NEGOTIATING
IN CHINA

36 STRATEGIES

NEGOTIATING IN CHINA

36 STRATEGIES

三十六计

Laurence J. Brahm

NAGA
GROUP LIMITED

南龍集團有限公司

B/H ASIA

Published by
Reed Academic Publishing Asia,
a division of Reed International (Singapore) Pte Ltd.
37 Jalan Pemimpin, Union Industrial Building,
Block B, #07-05, Singapore 2057.

© Laurence J. Brahm
First published 1995

ISBN 981-00-6606-6

Cover design by Heymans Tho, Sellgraphic
Typeset by Semantic Graphic Services
Printed in Singapore by KHL Printing Co Pte Ltd

CONTENTS

Contents

ABOUT THE COVER

The calligraphy of *"Thirty-six Strategies"* (三十六计) displayed on the cover of this book was prepared and presented to the author by Li Duo, one of China's most renown calligraphers and scholars of Chinese military strategy.

Li Duo (李铎) is recognized nationally as one of China's master calligraphers. Today he holds the position of Research Professor of the China People's Revolutionary Military Museum, as well as Vice Chairman of the China National Calligrapher's Association. His works are prized and collected by many of China's most important State leaders.

Li Duo today also serves as the Honorary Chairman of the Sun Bin (son of Sun Tze) Calligraphy and Painting Institute. He is also an Advisor to the China National Application of Sun Tze's Art of War Consulting Centre. In honor of Sun Tze's strategic philosophy, Master Li personally prepared a 200 metre long calligraphy of "Sun Tze's Art of War" which has since been engraved in stone. The stone engravings are currently protected in the China People's Revolutionary Military Museum and in Luoyang.

ABOUT THE AUTHOR

AUTHOR
Laurence J. Brahm is a director and legal advisor of the Naga Group.
He specialises in structuring and advising on China investments. He
divides his time between the Naga Group's Beijing, Shanghai, and Hong
Kong offices, negotiating investments on behalf of foreign multinationals.

EDITOR
Wing K. Yung is an advisor to the Naga Group. He specialises in matters
relating to China's economic and political development.

CONTRIBUTOR
Wang Bang Min is legal advisor to the Naga Group and a specialist on
Chinese administrative and economic law affairs. Formerly an official with
the Supreme People's Procuratorate, he is based in the Naga Group's
Beijing office.

ACKNOWLEDGEMENTS

For the uninitiated, negotiations in China may be a culture shock, iced with frustration. For the experienced China trade negotiator, it is a never-ending learning process.

In combining the classical with the existential, we have attempted to present a philosophical basis for defining one's mental composure prior to commencing negotiations in China.

In completing such an undertaking, I would like to express particular thanks to a number of individuals without whose assistance the completion of this book would not have been possible.

I would like to especially thank Wang Bang Min of Naga Group's Beijing office for his enormous work in researching the classical aspects of this book, and Wing Yung of Naga's Group Hong Kong office for his enormous advice in exploring the more philosophical aspects of the book.

I would also like to express my thanks to the administrative staff of Naga Group's Hong Kong and Beijing offices, especially Vera Wan for handling all administrative aspects of this publication, and to Catherine Law and Janet Yan for their assistance with the text.

Laurence J. Brahm
June, 1995
Beijing

FOREWORD

Cigarette smoke whirled to the ceiling filling the room like incense in a Taoist temple. Chessboard silence filled that space of the room not already consumed with cigarette smoke. In fact, one could hear the sound of a tea leaf unfolding and expanding in one of the porcelain teacups as piping hot water was poured from an aluminium flask.

The foreign party's financial controller hammered away at a plastic calculator. Their lawyer's Mont Blanc pen scratched across a sheet of paper. Somebody on the Chinese side of the table burped. Someone else snored.

The negotiators had been at it since 8:00 a.m. that morning. Nobody had left the room all day. Half-eaten club sandwiches and plates of Hainanese chicken rice lay spattered across the room. One of the foreign negotiators stood up and looked out the window of the top floor of this five-star hotel conference room at the traffic whizzing around one of Beijing's ring roads below. It was already dark. He whispered to his colleagues, "When will this be over?... Do you think we will be able to sign this year?"

Finally the foreign lawyer interrupted the silence. "Gentlemen, I think we have finally reached a point of general consensus on this one important issue. Now we can begin discussing the details of how it should be carried out. Then we can begin to re-word the contract language."

"In Chinese or in English?" asked the spokesman from the other side.

Negotiating in China has been described by many as a long and drawn-out process — one which demands patience, a known Confucian virtue; persistence, something which comes with time; and survival instincts — something acquired through persistence.

In this era of China's "Four Modernisations", many foreign negotiators are realising that the "way" to negotiating in China may be best sought from the source — China's ancient military classics.

Sun Tze's *Art of War* written about 2,000 years ago is the classic of classics, the ultimate guru's statement of military strategy, which can be applied to all levels of war, negotiation and life. It was the basis of much of Mao Zedong's writings on guerilla warfare in the 1940s, and has become the favourite textbook topic of a number of professors writing on business strategy in the 1990s.

The *Thirty-six Strategies* is a collection of thirty-six sayings which capsulise thirty-six stories of strategic prowess in ancient Chinese history. Most of these stories are derived from military ploys applied during the Warring States Period (403–221 BC) or during the Three Kingdom Period (220–265 BC).

Together, Sun Tze's *Art of War* and the *Thirty-six Strategies* have become a part of the collective unconscious of most educated Chinese. From childhood, the strategies of Sun Tze and the *Thirty-six Strategies* are learned in school, in literature, and even in popular folk opera, and sometimes on CCTV television serials.

To negotiate in China without at least a cursory knowledge of Sun Tze's *Art of War* and the *Thirty-six Strategies* is like walking into a minefield without a map.

This book attempts to apply Sun Tze's *Art of War* and the *Thirty-six Strategies* to actual negotiating situations in China, both commercial and diplomatic. This book is written for the uninitiated (those who have had little negotiating experience in China) as well as the over-initiated (those who have been negotiating in China for some time and may be suffering from an overdose). In either case, the reader should be able to relate to the stories contained herein.

The stories in this book are based on fact. This book is written with the intention to provide some amusement, and maybe hope, when one is staring out of the window of a China hotel business centre conference room, watching the traffic, and wondering "When will they sign?".

GLOSSARY OF TERMS

The following are useful terms which one may encounter in their negotiations in China and in the text of this book.

Maotai :
（茅台）

A fiery white rice wine which is kept in stone bottles because it eats through glass; a favourite liquor used for toasts at Chinese banquets.

Baole :
（饱了）

A feeling literally translated as "I'm stuffed" which is uttered at various stages of discomfort during a banquet when one is consuming a wide menagerie of ducks, snakes, pigeons, turtles, abalone, and just about anything else which one might remember as a kid when visiting the zoo.

Ganbei :
（干杯）

An action best defined as "bottoms up"; to be performed after a long and complimentary toast; to be followed by showing one's guests the empty glass as proof that all the liquor has been drunk and as an expression of one's friendship and tolerance.

Bonding :

A popular MBA yuppy buzz word which in China means sitting around the karaoke bar until 2:00 a.m. *ganbei*ing one glass of XO after another with one's Chinese counterparts.

Post-Bonding Syndrome :

Vomitting all the XO and menagerie over one's bed in the hotel room at 3:00 a.m. after a successful bonding session.

Courtesan :

A maid in waiting at the Emperor's court during either the Three Kingdoms or Warring States Period; someone who wears lots of make-up and is equipped with beeper and handphone; a person who knocks at your hotel room door at 2:30 a.m. when you have just returned from a successful bonding session and are about to begin post-bonding syndrome.

Friendly
negotiations : A state of euphoria which is often not as friendly as one would like to believe.
（友好协商）

Get me a ticket
to Hong Kong : A statement which one should remember how to say in Chinese.
（请帮我买机
票回香港）

Strategic Planning : For western negotiators, this involves complex coordination between various corporate departments and the analysis of findings from various in-depth studies of the China market carried out by top-line international consulting groups culminating in pre-negotiation strategic briefing sessions and post-negotiation strategic de-briefing sessions; For Chinese negotiators, this means applying any of the 36 strategies set out in Part IV of this book!

Sun Tze :
（曹操） Literally translated as "Master Sun"; the guru of strategy; a Chinese military master and philosopher who lived 2,000 years ago; the most popular name to use on the title of an MBA textbook.

Cao Cao :
（孙子） A hero of the Three Kingdoms period. "When you least expect him, he is there".
（"说曹操，曹操就到。"）

Three Kingdoms : A novel which is actually more a history of three kingdoms (Wei, Wu and Shu) which fought against each other a little less than 2,000 years ago, and have become the basis for many strategies contained in this book.

Glossary of Terms

Warring States : A period of Chinese history when everyone fought against everyone else; not to be confused with your joint venture's board of directors meeting.

XO : A semi-sweet cognac which is supposed to be "extra old" thereby being dubbed "XO"; a favourite liquor used for toasts in karaoke bars; a necessity to be purchased at the Duty Free shop before entering China on a negotiation trip.

Mutual understanding （互相了解） : A feeling of disbelief if it can be believed; something like Nirvana which is rarely attained.

Introduction

THE ANATOMY OF A NEGOTIATION IN CHINA

Friendship and Mutual Understanding (友谊与相互利用)

"Yes" is always the first word of negotiation not the last in China. Too often when foreign investors and businessmen hear the word "yes" in China, they assume that the deal is done. In fact, it is only the beginning of what may often be a long and protracted negotiation process.

"Sleeping in the same bed and dreaming different dreams" (同床异梦) is an ancient Chinese saying which reflects two thousand years of experience with partners who may have their own dreams but are willing to share temporary accommodations in order to get what they want — and then leave. This is too often the problem with business deals in China. Both parties have completely different internal motivations of what they want out of the deal. Thus, both parties end up getting into bed together on a joint venture and find that they are stuck — with a bad marriage.

The process of entering into a joint venture in China is like getting married. The parties will first sign a "letter of intent" which is a non-legally binding document which serves more as an expression of seriousness that the two parties wish to form a joint venture. This document is something like an engagement ring.

The marriage will be solemnised when the parties actually enter into a joint venture contract. Before entering into a joint venture contract, that is the stage between signing the letter of intent and signing the contract, the parties will undertake together a feasibility study to make sure that the marriage makes real financial sense and that it is not all just hype and romance. Deals often simply fall apart at this stage. While western businessmen often think that the Chinese joint venture marital process is bureaucratic, it is usually very practical when viewed from this perspective.

When the business licence is finally issued by the relevant authorities, the marriage is a sealed deal and the only way out is divorce — or arbitration.

Frontline Negotiations (当面谈判)

Negotiations in China can be characterised as taking place on two different levels:

- public level (or frontline negotiations),
- private level (or backdoor liaison).

The frontline negotiations are what take place in the boardroom, or the smoke-filled conference room of a hotel business centre. These are the negotiations which take place on a public level, that is everyone is present and everyone has something (or too much for that matter) to say. This is why frontline negotiations can take a long time and become protracted negotiations — that is if someone doesn't get smart and use the backdoor liaison approach.

Frontline negotiations are in MBA talk "process-oriented". That means they take a long time. To some extent that is a good thing because only by being patient and taking a long time can both sides really understand what the other side actually means or wants. Putting it all down in the contract is another thing because it is not always so easy to reflect what both sides want in two different languages and get it right at the first shot. This all takes time and more patience. Thus we can call frontline negotiations a "process-oriented" occupation.

The Chinese are always characterised as being tough bargainers. This is because "face" is always an issue of concern. "Face" is a concept which cannot be translated into any western language but which is something similar to respect, honour, fairness, equality and recognition of all these things together. A westerner can only begin to understand "face" when he has had to face the issue of "face" enough times so that the concept sinks in. The idea is to give your Chinese counterpart "face" at the negotiation table without losing it yourself.

The Chinese party will also always talk as if they are safeguarding the interests of their company, enterprise, or nation when negotiating with you, especially when there are many people at the negotiation table. This is clearly an aspect of the public level of negotiating. When one thinks that their counterparts are safeguarding the interests of a State enterprise in the atmosphere of a collapsing State enterprise system in a booming market economy and inflation of over twenty percent, one wonders how much the other party is really fighting for the company or nation's interest.

Backdoor Liaison (走后门)

While negotiations in China often appear to be process-oriented, the Chinese party always has a distinct set of objectives in hand. In this regard, negotiations can be purely goal-oriented if one is able to find out what the Chinese party's actual objectives are and address them. This however, will never come out on the table in a formal negotiation at the public level. One must therefore find someone on the other side of the table they can pull out of the room, or meet on a purely personal level to find out what the other side really wants.

Western businessmen too often worry about formal presentations and stiff shirt and tie personal decor, and generally being uptight about business as is expected in the west and taught in MBA courses in such towering citadels of learning such as Harvard and Oxford. Such towering learning dosen't get one as far along in China as learning how to drink, smoke and sing karaoke songs, which can actually pull the negotiations out of a deadpass situation and bring it onto a personal level, where the Chinese party may actually open up and reveal what is really on their mind.

More negotiating is done in dance halls and karaoke rooms in China than at the formal negotiating table. Furthermore, the Chinese like to know who they are getting into bed with on a business deal on a personal level. As from the practical operational point of view, if the relationship isn't there, then it dosen't matter how sharply the figures balance. In a Chinese context, the parties have to get along together before they can work together.

Meanwhile, while the Chinese are chanting about benefit to company and country, it is in moments of relaxed revelry that one will get them to disclose what's really on their mind and what they really want out of the deal, that is the benefit to them as individuals — and you better believe that there is a benefit somewhere — and how that benefit can be best addressed.

Likewise, while the enterprise managers have their immediate goals — which are usually in the form of cash — the government cadres to whom they report have their own set of goals, which usually run something like, "How much investment can I get into my province or city?, how fast and how big can the projects be or at least seem to the cadres above me?"

Through the right type of "backdoor" liaison, one can if necessary upon finding what the cadres want, use this to leverage the enterprise managers with pressure from above. Likewise, you can use the cadres below if they won't budge, and by going continually upwards leverage more pressure downwards, and so on.

The problem is when someone goes too far up the political lobbying process that they lose touch with the people who they still have to live with at the end of the day — mainly their partners and the local government officials — that the whole lobbying process gets out of proportion.

Many multinationals think that all their problems can be solved by getting an audience with Li Peng or Zhu Rongji. This is clearly the wrong approach, as these individuals have so much on their hands, that the last thing they will get excited about is every single investment project which is brought to their attention. Furthermore, getting the top officials to approve a project does not mean that the bureaucrats below will budge quickly. The days of Mao Zedong uttering a few words and everyone coming to attention are more or less over. Nevertheless, good relations at the national level can help. The point is that one needs good relations at all levels in order to get things done effectively.

Part I

ENTER THE DRAGON:
THE ETIQUETTE OF
WHAT TO DO
AND NOT DO
WHEN MEETING PRC OFFICIALS

"When Entering the Province, One Should Follow the Customs" (入乡随俗)

The fried scorpions sat delicately on a bed of rice noodles. Their pincers were open. Their eyes looked questionably at the ceiling.

"Try one," offered the Chinese host.

His western counterpart, a refined and respected American businessman, grimaced.

"He is the Minister," reminded the businessman's Chinese assistant who was the company's Beijing office representative. The businessman shakily used his chopsticks to pick one fine fried scorpion up from the centre plate by the tail. "You do want the deal, don't you?" his Chinese assistant reminded him. Hearing those words — and with eyes closed — he shoved the whole fried scorpion down his throat, and let it melt in his mouth. (For the uninitiated, a fried scorpion tastes like a fried silk worm — albeit more delicate and crunchy.)

Proper table etiquette can open or close doors in China. In other words, do not offend your host!

At the same time, western businessmen often cringe at local etiquette which they find offensive or simply do not understand — or appreciate. For instance, bear's paw is extremely expensive and one should eat their designated share if served one.

Likewise, drinking is also a critical part of the ceremony. It is not so important what one is drinking so much as the fact that they are drinking a lot of it and swallowing it in entire cupfuls.

Ganbei (干杯) means "bottoms up." A proper *ganbei* toast begins with a short speech of above five minutes discoursing the friendship between the two parties, governments, or individuals, honorific mention of everybody else at the table regardless of how friendly they are to each other, and then pouring the contents of the glass down one's throat. This is then followed by showing everyone present the empty glass as evidence of the fact that you drank the contents thereby consecrating the subject of the speech.

8

One China hand, in order to get through prolonged banquets in successive days practised a number of sleight of hand tricks — namely pouring the contents of the glass under the table or over his shoulder when everyone was distracted. Unfortunately, this backfired when on one occasion, he kept hitting the back of the dress of one of the senior cadre host's wife, sitting at the table behind him.

So if your host tops up your cup with fiery Maotai or your water glass with XO, and proposes a toast screaming *ganbei* to the chagrin of all the waiters, it is best for you to down whatever is in the glass. Excessive rounds of *ganbei* (often mixing first Maotai, then Cognac, then white wine, then beer, and then back to the Maotai) often sends even the stoutest western businessman reeling his way to the men's room.

One must therefore adopt a flexible attitude when embarking on the social aspects of doing a China deal — especially when dining with the power elites who could make or break — in other words, approve — your deal.

The classic case of diplomatic etiquette occurred shortly after the warming of China-US relations, when Theodore White (who was a journalist covering the Red Army during the war against the KMT) returned to China to see his old friend, then Premier Zhou Enlai. At the banquet, a roast suckling pig was brought to the table.

"I can't eat this," exclaimed White, "I am Kosher!"

Premier Zhou Enlai, always the courteous diplomat, placed his arm around White and pointing at the table, explained in a gentle voice, "But look twice Teddy, it is REALLY a Peking Duck!"

"The Dog Acts Fierce when the Master is Present"
(狗仗人势)

Addressing your counterpart in formal discussions is another mark of etiquette and education in China. While China may be a classless society under Communism, some observers have noted that it is also one of the most hierarchical societies in the world today.

Chinese officials meet foreigners who are their equivalent in stature and rank. So if your company's CEO and President wishes to meet a Minister or even Vice Premier, then this may be possible to arrange. But if it is the Deputy CEO or Vice President, then he will have to be resigned to meeting a Deputy Minister.

Many CEOs of foreign multinationals still have the days of Kissinger and Zhou Enlai at the back of their minds when they go to China, when what Mao said was, and that was simply all there was to it. They think that the China market can be opened to them as simply as US-China normalisation could be had on the back of a handshake between Mao and Nixon. This kind of thinking is to say the least a big mistake.

"If we can get a meeting between our company's President and Zhu Rongji, will we be able to get approval for everything we want and open up the China market?" asked one US multinational's Hong Kong manager (who had been supervising his company's activities in China for years). Unlikely scenario. In fact, the most someone like Zhu Rongji would say to a foreign multinational's CEO would be (and that is under the best of circumstances), "Please come to invest in China. We welcome you to invest in China. As long as you invest in accordance with ALL OF CHINA'S RELEVANT LAWS AND CONCERNED POLICIES, we will encourage and support you coming to China to invest."

The key catchword is of course "all of China's relevant laws and concerned policies." You will hear these words when your CEO meets with State leaders. Remember, these words are very important. They mean that you should open up the China law books and find out what the policies are. You should then go back to square one and invest in accordance with all the procedures that you are supposed to follow starting from ground floor and working your way up. No shortcuts available on the back of a photo session with Zhu Rongji.

The fad over the past year has been for the CEOs of US multinationals to fly to Beijing to meet with Ministers and Vice Premiers to "tell the Chinese to stop playing games and open up their markets." (This of course ignores the fact that the IMF has now rated China as having a more free and open trading system than that of the US, and the World Bank has rated China as being the third largest economy in the world behind only Japan and the US itself.) In any event, many CEOs, frustrated with lack of productivity at home, flew to China last year and had meetings with Chinese officials (many of whom responded that it is not China's responsibility to solve America's unemployment problems).

In short, opening the China market is not that difficult. There are many Hong Kong, Taiwan, Singaporean, Japanese and Korean companies that have been very successful at this without sending their CEOs in for high-powered horn-locking sessions with China's leaders, who are busier trying to undertake national economic reform and massive infrastructure development while containing inflation — not an easy balancing act by anyone's standards — to be terribly concerned that the Chinese are not buying enough US manufactured cars, cameras and Christmas cards.

"Obedience is Better than a Show of Respect"
（恭敬不如从命）

Proper translators in meetings with high-level officials can help set the tone — or create discord. Usually when meeting with an official, the parties will assemble in the main conference or reception room of the Ministry of Bureau concerned. There will be a row of chairs on one side for the foreign party to sit on. There will be another row of chairs on the other side for the Chinese party to sit on. There will be two chairs presiding at the end of the room for the head of the foreign delegation and the highest ranking official from the Chinese party. Behind each of these two individuals will be small seats for the translators to sit on.

It is best in meetings such as this for the foreign party to make sure that the Chinese official has been well briefed by his assistants as to what the real purpose of the meeting is. Otherwise meetings will ramble on without any consequence and be overtaken with niceties, without ever getting to the point.

It is often customary when meeting officials formally, to follow the formal meeting with a banquet. One particular provincial governor was well-known for his capacity to drink enormous amounts of alcohol at banquets. When arranging the formal meeting with his staff, they asked the foreign delegation's liaison, "We know you are paying for the banquet, but do you want to organise the venue or should we?"

The foreign delegation's leader however, was very upset emphasising that the delegation.flew all the way to China to meet with this provincial governor to straighten out a problem. "We came to China to be serious. Enough of this drinking and eating. We are going to be serious. I want a formal and serious meeting with the Governor."

Everyone filed into the Provincial Governor's office and sat stoically. The foreign delegation's leader began to go into a long diatribe concerning their problems in the province. After fifteen minutes, the Governor in a sweeping gesture with his hand, interrupted the foreign team's spokesman and exclaimed, "OK! I support you to invest in my province. Now we go to the banquet for drinking!"

Careful translation can make or break such meetings with high-ranking officials. Take for instance the historical meeting between Nixon and Mao's wife, Jiang Qing. Nixon was accompanied by one of Harvard University's best-educated Chinese translators. When Nixon shook Madame Mao's hand he exclaimed, "Madame Mao you are very beautiful." She replied politely, "Nali Nali" (哪里哪里), which is to indicate that Nixon was flattering her too much. The Harvard translator however, provided a literal translation of "where where," leaving Nixon completely confused.

Part II

THE ART OF
NEGOTIATING IN CHINA

China Hands (老中国通)

It was not just another "China conference" in a five-star hotel in Hong Kong. It was the China conference, held at a five-star hotel in Shanghai. Everyone who was supposed to be seen in the China trade was there.

The economists were there in their grey flannel jackets. The accountants were there wearing designer glasses with lenses as thick as the bottom of Coca Cola bottles. The merchant bankers were there with their suspenders and gold pins through their collars. And of course, circling around the rest like sharks moving in for the kill, were the lawyers from all of the top law firms in their black three-piece suits looking to crack the China market.

The first speaker of the morning was the economist. He proceeded to draw his theory on the board and explain that his theory concerning the growth of the Chinese economy was assumptions, and therefore, it must be accurate.

The accountant who came next, was from one of the top accounting firms. He proceeded to explain that when their firm prepares a feasibility study for a China deal, it is carried out with the greatest of thorough detail and that all of the statistics which they develop for the feasibility study are most accurate because they are all based on the economist's theory which is based on a solid set of assumptions, and therefore, it must be accurate too.

The accountant was followed by the merchant banker whose suspenders held up his pants over bulges formed from the consumption of martinis and fine foods served in five-star hotels and first class sections of airlines. The merchant banker proceeded to explain how his merchant bank was best placed to handle "China deals" because their China team had dozens of merchant bankers who travelled widely and stayed in a variety of five-star hotels in China and therefore they all knew China very well. By the way, they did flotation and bond issues and they would even tie your shoes for you if you gave them enough money. After

14

this discourse, the merchant banker explained that their secret to success was that in every "China deal", they would, for a vast sum of money, form for the client, a special strategic entry model which would be based on a series of hypothesis which were always accurate because these hypothesis were based on very accurate statistics formed by the best of the accountants and these statistics could not be wrong because they were based on a well-founded theory which was based on a solid set of assumptions, and therefore, if one paid for their hypothesis, one would never go wrong entering the China market, of course.

Then it was the lawyer's turn to speak. The lawyer glared at the audience in his three-piece black suit and told the audience that in view of the China entry strategy formed by the merchant bankers on the basis of the hypothesis which was based on the statistics prepared by the accountants which were based on the theory prepared by the economists which was based on a very solid set of assumptions, that it would be absolutely necessary to put all of this into the contract and that when negotiating with the Chinese party, every single detail of all of these points would have to be spelled out correctly in the contract, and god forbid if there was any oversight, and every single i in the contract would have to be dotted and every single t crossed, and there would need to be at least 40 drafts to get it right, and they should all be reviewed by half-a-dozen partners, followed by at least a dozen assistant lawyers and their entourage of at least two dozen clerks. And of course all of this had to be done correctly, and charged by the hour.

The last speaker of the day was not an economist, accountant, merchant banker, or lawyer. In fact, the last speaker of the day was not a professional at all. He was simply the foreign manager of a joint venture in China. He arrived in China three years before to negotiate the joint venture at which time he spoke no Chinese. However, by the time of the conference, three years later, he had already learned to speak fluent Chinese, having worked on the plant of the joint venture with the local workers every day since the joint venture was established.

The manager looked at the white board in the conference room with all the assumptions, theories, statistics, hypothesis, and all the dotted i's and all the crossed t's. He looked at the white board with interest and simply said, "Well, when we did our joint venture, it didn't happen like this at all. In fact, it was quite simple. After days of negotiating, the room was filled with cigarette smoke, there were burnt cigarettes overflowing every ashtray and coffee-cup saucer. Finally, in the heat of the last afternoon, the translator burped, somebody misinterpreted what she said, the other party put forward the misinterpretation, we all liked it, everybody agreed, and everyone was so happy that we finally found consensus on an issue that everybody decided to have a banquet. We then went to the karaoke bar and drank XO until 2:00 a.m. in the morning when the management threw us out. The next morning when we got together, everyone was in such a good mood, that we signed everything right away. Later, we had the translators fix up the language so it could all be approved by the government. Within three months, we had our business licence and were into production." Silence filled the room.

Sleeping in the Same Bed But Dreaming Different Dreams (同床异梦)

When negotiating in China, the first rule is not to bring your lawyer along. The second is to throw away your MBA textbook. The third is to listen to what the other party has to say.

Too many western businessmen fill their minds with preconceptions and spend too much time with their lawyers and accountants trying to figure out elaborate entry strategies and complicated business deals to present to the Chinese party. After all the preparation and the internal corporate complications, they meet with the Chinese party only to find that the Chinese party has a completely different agenda. "We really don't want your technology any more. All we want is cash!"

Much can be learned from the Chinese saying "to sleep in the same bed but dream different dreams." Most of the reasons for breakdowns in joint venture negotiations, or breakups in joint ventures after the deal is sealed, is because the two parties who have decided to get into the same bed have dreams that are fundamentally different.

Each party has its own set of objectives, its own goals. These however, may be totally different. The foreign party may want to invest in what it thinks will be a great real estate project with long-term financial rewards, while the Chinese partner may only be interested in squeezing as much money as possible out of the costs being paid by the foreign party to remove the existing tenants off the land.

The foreign party may be brimming over with enthusiasm over its joint venture with a Chinese State-owned detergent factory (given China's enormous domestic savings and growing urban consumer market, and so on and so forth) thinking that with their foreign technology the Chinese party will welcome the opportunity to make the old State-owned factory superefficient. The Chinese party however, may be more interested in diverting the compensation being paid to lay off useless and redundant workers into setting up other businesses, which they see as being more profitable in the long run.

Likewise, the foreign party may be busy sending its whizz-kid MBA type marketing people to do elaborate surveys of the China market so as to impress everyone with fanciful overhead slide presentations in board-room meetings, while its Chinese partner is more interested in finding practical tricks and under-the-counter methods of getting the joint venture's products shelf space on the competitive Shanghai and Beijing markets (while at the same time trying to find similar ways of keeping the competitor's products off the shelf!).

Consequently, it is critical to understand your partner in China, and to make sure that your partner understands you. Otherwise, if you find that you have been "sleeping in the same bed while dreaming different dreams," then you may realise — too late — that you should have been in separate beds all along.

The Art of Saying "Yes" (说 "是" 的艺术)

One of the problems faced by the westerner dealing in China is that of basic communication. For the western businessmen, "yes" means that the deal is done, and the contracts can be signed, and if anything goes wrong you can always sue on the contract. Right? Wrong — at least in China.

In China, "yes" is the first word of negotiations, not the last. For the Chinese, "yes" means let's sit down and talk seriously. The flow of western businessmen who have come back to Hong Kong excitedly exclaiming that they have a "done deal" is unfathomable.

"They (the Chinese) said 'yes' you know. The mayor of the city was there too. He kept nodding his head throughout the banquet, therefore he must have liked our idea and agreed. The factory manager also said 'no problem' so that means that everyone must be in agreement. Let's get the contracts ready and go back and sign them up before they change their mind."

Good luck!

When the Chinese say "yes" in negotiations, there is a very fine art of understanding to what degree they actually agree to what the foreign party is saying. For instance, when the Chinese respond during negotiations by saying:

- *ming bai* (明白) they mean that they understood what the foreign party just said;
- *ke yi* (可以) they mean that anything the foreign party is proposing is possible;
- *tong yi* (同意) they mean that they actually agree to the point made by the foreign party.
- *dui* (对), there is a range of broad literal meanings ranging from "OK", "Yeah", "Sure", "Why not", "I see", "Ah-so", "Ah-ha".

Anything short of *tong yi* means that there is no deal. Beware of the fact that *ming bai*, *ke yi*, *tong yi* and *dui* can all be loosely translated as "yes."

During one negotiation, the foreign party prepared all the documents, and the Chinese party went off to their hotel room to read them. Finally the General Manager of the foreign party telephoned the Chinese party and asked if there was any problem.

The Chinese party's spokesman responded over the phone, "*Mei you wenti* (no problem)."

"Does that mean you are prepared to sign the documents?" asked the General Manager.

"*Ke yi* (possible)," responded the Chinese party's spokesman.

"Don't give me this *ke yi* stuff," the General Manager reacted. "Are you going to sign them or not?"

"*Ying gai ke yi* (most probably possible)," responded the Chinese party's spokesman.

"Don't give me this *ying gai ke yi* stuff either. Are you signing or not? Yes or no?" screamed the foreign General Manager.

"I'm not sure," replied the Chinese party's spokesman. "I better go back and ask my superior."

Contractual Protection (合同保护)

The western legal mindset understands a contract as a document which is legally binding and to which you have recourse should anything go wrong. In other words, if the other party "breaks" their side of the bargain, we can sue them and drag them through the courts. Right?

Welcome to China. Five million US dollars worth of equipment are bolted down to the factory floor in Szechuan province. The other five million is in a joint bank account with the Bank of China. The foreign trademarks are all under licence to the joint venture and the moulds are in Szechuan province too. There is a management conflict and the foreign party wants to take recourse on the terms of the contract through the courts. The courts are out because this is not in line with Chinese practice so arbitration is the only option. If the foreign party wins, then this means that the lawyers get congratulated and paid. Then, try and sort out the rest. Who is then going to go to the factory and get the machines unbolted, on a train, through customs and out of the country? Certainly not the lawyer.

Is the fault with the Chinese? No, the fault is with the western party who insists on adopting a western legalistic approach to the practical realities of doing business in China. What works in law school or in the boardroom of the executive offices of the finest blue chip law firm has little relevance to making a factory in rural China work, and even less relevance to making the people on the other side of the negotiation table understand what the foreign party actually wants to do with the factory once the contract is signed and approved.

What is critical to understand in negotiating a contract is that the contract should be viewed as a tool by which both parties can assure that the other party understands what they understand, and everybody knows what they have to put into the deal to make it work, and what everyone will get out at the end of the day if it does work. This is the essence of the importance of a legal contract in China. One does not want to focus their attention on the legalities of "what will happen if," that is if one really wants to get the deal. Rather the contract should be the tool by which one rests assure that everyone understands everyone else so that no disputes will arise at all and the deal can work and everyone will work together to achieve that goal.

The foreigners who buzz into China on a whirlwind, anxious to sign up documents on the belief that if everything is legal and covered in the contract that they can go to court or arbitration if something goes wrong, are missing the whole point of doing business in China. Those foreigners who spend a lot of time with their Chinese counterparts and understand how they think and what they want, and find a way that everyone can make everything happen for everyone else, and communicate these ideas through clear language in à contract, will be solidifying not just the deal but a long-term business relationship which is what business in China is all about in the first place.

20

Developing a Legal System — From Scratch (法律保护)

When one British merchant banker in Hong Kong exclaimed, "There is no law in China, so how can you do business with the people where they have no law?", he demonstrated both his arrogance and ignorance to everyone in the boardroom.

China has developed a legal system, largely geared for foreign investors, from scratch. Starting in 1979, China adopted its "Equity Joint Venture Law" on the back of the open door policy which was marked by Deng Xiaoping's ascendancy to power at the 11th Party Congress in 1978.

Since that time, China has adopted legislation for equity as well as co-operative joint ventures, wholly foreign-owned investment enterprises, and complete legislation governing all aspects of intellectual property, foreign exchange control, and dispute resolution. In the past few years, China has put in place legislation to govern securities markets, and recently has adopted a Corporate Law.

Within just thirteen years, China has adopted enough legislation so as to have a legal system as complete as just about any other country. Within thirteen years, China has undertaken legal reforms which took Europe some five centuries.

The problem with western businessmen is that they do not understand how the Chinese legal system works, and how it can benefit them.

Laws passed by the National People's Congress set forth general principles which are implemented through subsequent detailed rules and regulations promulgated by the State Council (the executive branch of the government) or by the particular ministry, commission, or bureau concerned. One should look to the law for the general principles, the rules and regulations for the details of how the principles should be applied, and any circulars or notices for the leftover details which may be still missing or unclear.

This system makes enormous sense for a developing country with an economy undergoing fundamental transformations. The law sets the parameters, but following an assessment of the situation (to be read as "reaction of the people") the government will fill the gaps with implementing legislation.

What one needs to be aware of is the shifting policies which often underwrite the law. Understanding these policies means understanding how the government thinks. This way, one can understand the underlying reason for limitations in the law and play this to one's ultimate advantage in structuring a deal which works practically. In Chinese, Taoist philosophy, water always flows down the path of least resistance.

Protracted Negotiations (长期谈判)

Often foreign parties are frustrated at the prolonged nature of negotiations in China which are often considered to be long and protracted, something like a guerilla warfare. This is because to some extent, the Chinese will adopt every kind of psychological and even physical tactics to wear down the negotiating team on the other side of the table.

In fact, negotiations begin the moment the foreign team enters China. Controlling the other party's schedule is fundamental to the Chinese negotiating process.

On one visit, the foreign negotiating team may be met by their counterparts in the airport and escorted with red carpet treatment through customs. One another visit, they may be left outside the airport, without car or guide, until "found" by their counterpart.

The foreign team may arrive in China hot to hit the negotiation table only to find that their hosts have planned a full sightseeing tour for their guests to look at all the old temples and pagodas remaining in the city, followed by a full banquet, which leaves the foreign negotiating team exhausted and stuffed, with the lean Chinese team ready to begin negotiations at 7:00 a.m. the next day.

And when negotiations drag on without resolution, the place to move is outside of the negotiating room. The Chinese place great importance on harmony in relations. Friendship is paramount. Banquets with many toasts will warm up the atmosphere. The real deal can often be done in the karaoke bar over XO, when everyone feels a little less tense, and issues can be discussed frankly. If one listens closely enough, the Chinese party may, in such circumstances, tell you exactly what the problem is and what needs to be done to clear it up so that everyone can move on to the next stage of discussions.

As one negotiator commented, "If you do the deal too quickly, they will think something is wrong. So when they want to take you to see the Great Wall, then stop pounding your fist on the table and just go along." Sometimes, the path of least resistance covers the most ground.

Knowing Your Counterpart (知己知披)

The worst mistake that anyone can make in a negotiation is to underestimate the opposition. The Chinese party may not look as slick as their foreign western counterparts, but they may know a lot more about the west than the westerners know about China. During the late seventies, China was coming out of the Cultural Revolution and during the eighties, into a new era of economic growth. In those days, western imports were new and westerners found it easy business to impress their counterparts.

The China of the 1990s is different. The Chinese have adopted a new kind of sophistication which goes along with being the third largest economy in the world (according to the IMF), and being among the top six nations in the world to possess the highest levels of foreign exchange reserves. Chinese-backed corporations are now unabashedly issuing bonds and listing on all the major markets of the world.

Today, these corporations are adopting unique management style which can best be described as "market socialism with 'Chinese' characteristics." Once upon a time, a foreign negotiator could impress his counterparts by offering a packet of Marlboro cigarettes and exclaiming, "American cigarettes are number one." The last time this author saw a fast-talking American try to pull this move, the Chinese factory director responded by graciously accepting the packet. He then paused, snapped his fingers and ordered his secretary, "Mei Ling, bring out the Davidoff cigars and Remy Martin Club for our guest."

As one Chinese friend explained, "You see, when foreigners hear about Deng Xiaoping's 'market socialism with Chinese characteristics', they think it is just another one of the Party's jingles. They simply continue to miss the whole point. You see, market socialism in China has CHINESE characteristics!"

Part III

SUN TZE'S:
ART OF NEGOTIATING
IN CHINA

Getting Started

"He who knows the art of the direct and the indirect approach will be victorious. Such is the art of manoeuvring."
（先知迂直之计者胜。 此军争之法也。）

Sun Tze

"Yes" in China may be the first word of agreement, but not always the last word in negotiations. "Yes" is often simply another way of saying, "Let's begin to talk seriously." The Chinese often interpret the conclusion of a contract to mean that the two parties now understand each other well enough to begin asking for further favours.

What may be viewed as simply a favour to one party may seem like a costly concession to the other. For the Western party, a contract is a contract and the obligations of the parties are those obligations spelled out therein. Western culture is goal-oriented: Negotiations are simply a process through which the final goal — the contract — is reached.

Chinese society is process-oriented. Consequently, for the Chinese, negotiations often involve understandings and intentions not spelled out in the final contract. These can resurface at any time, often couched in phrases like, "Based on our friendship and mutual understanding, could you please...". Because of Confucian values and the Chinese emphasis on interpersonal relations, these requests may have nothing to do with the contract terms at all, and range from things like, "Can you get my kid into an American college to study?" to "Our company/factory would like a new Mercedes Benz."

Despite the emphasis on interpersonal relations, the Chinese are tough negotiators. Western businessmen often find contract negotiations in China to be a traumatic, stressful endurance test. Chinese negotiating tactics have been best described as being analogous to guerrilla warfare: "Strike hard, retreat, seize a position, reject compromise, and strike again."

Should it be surprising that such tactics are used? Strategic philosophy has a long history in China. Chinese leaders, both political and military, from Cao Cao of the Three Kingdoms period to Mao Zedong of modern times, have looked to a Machiavellian philosophy recorded by Sun Wu (known to the world as "Sun Tze" or "Master Sun") in his treatise, *Art of War*, more than 2,000 years ago.

In a sense, Sun Tze's *Art of War*, like other writings from China's classical period, has worked its way into the collective subconscious of Chinese diplomatic thinking. It is not hard to see how the strategies propounded by Sun Tze are directly applicable to the negotiating style characterised by China's negotiators today.

The Strategical Attack

"Keep him under strain and wear him down."
（佚而劳之）

Sun Tze

For Western businesspersons, a negotiation in China may seem like a protracted guerrilla warfare. This is because the Chinese use every possible psychological and physiological ploy to wear down the opposite party. As Sun Tze wrote: "Attack where he is unprepared; sally out where he does not expect you." In negotiations, this is precisely what the Chinese do.

It is often suggested that Western negotiators should be careful about the amount of tea they drink during negotiations, because discussions often drag on for hours without a break. While Western negotiations often include planned breaks, the Chinese see negotiations as a means of testing the opposition's resolve.

When coming to China for negotiations, Western businessmen should disregard their MBA textbooks and heed Sun Tze's advice that "invincibility depends on one's self; the enemy's vulnerability on himself." It follows that "those skilled ... can make themselves invincible but cannot cause an enemy to be...vulnerable."

One should not forget the mistakes of one British negotiator who made himself vulnerable by agreeing to remain in China and continue discussions over the Christmas holidays. He should have read Sun Tze. The Chinese had. They knew that the Christmas period would greatly reduce their opponent's resistance to pressure for concessions.

Opening Negotiations

> *"Ground which both we and the enemy can traverse with equal ease is called accessible. In such ground, he who first takes high sunny positions...can fight advantageously."*
>
> （我可以往，彼可以来，曰通。
>
> 通行者，先居高阳。。。从战则利。）
>
> Sun Tze

The Chinese open negotiations by trying to establish their own ground rules from the start. They do this by pressing their foreign counterparts to agree to certain general principles. The agreement to principles usually takes the form of a "letter of intent." To the Westerner, these principles may seem like ritual statements because they lack any kind of specific detail.

Be careful. One should not make too many assumptions regarding initial formalities. As Chang Yu wrote in his commentary on the *Art of War*: "If one should be the first to occupy a position on level ground, how much more does this apply to difficult and dangerous places!"

The Chinese understand this well. The principles initially agreed to, will set up a conceptual parameter within which the parties must work in order for discussions to progress. Later, the Chinese may invoke these principles to suggest that the foreign party has not lived up to the spirit of "mutual cooperation and benefit" initially agreed upon.

The Chinese emphasis on general principles strikes an unusual chord in Western businessmen. It is interesting to note that of the "five fundamental factors" of strategy, Sun Tze wrote that, "the first (most important) of

28

these factors is moral influence." The Chinese emphasis on the persuasion of general principles contrasts sharply with the Western notion of focusing on details and hammering out specifics in the narrow context of a legal framework.

The Pace of Negotiations

"When the enemy is at ease, be able to weary him; when well fed, to starve him; when at rest, to make him move."

（佚而劳之，饱而饥之，静而动之。）

Sun Tze

The Chinese like to dictate the pace of negotiations and the agenda. Little does the unwary Western businessman realise that real negotiating begins at the moment of arrival in China. In fact, the first-time visitor will feel he has really been caught off-guard.

"Appear at places to which he must hasten; move swiftly where he does not expect you," wrote Sun Tze. On one visit, a Western businessman may find his Chinese hosts waiting to greet him before going through customs. On another visit, the same businessman may have to wait outside in a milling airport crowd, until found by the representative of his host organisation. Regardless, even if the visitors take preparatory measures (e.g., book their own hotels in advance), their Chinese hosts ultimately control the schedule.

Controlling the other party's schedule gives the Chinese the element of surprise. Beware the visitor who arrives hot to hit the negotiating table. His hosts may have a few sightseeing tours (i.e. a full-day drive to the Great Wall and back, followed by a heavy Peking Duck dinner) in store for their jetlagged guest. "When I wish to avoid battle," wrote Sun Tze, "I may defend myself simply by drawing a line on the ground; the enemy will be unable to attack me because I divert him from going where he wishes."

As one Hong Kong merchandiser explained: "Whenever I state a final position and they (the Chinese) don't want to accept, they will respond by

29

saying, 'Young miss, young miss, don't get upset, let's go drink tea and have dim sum now,' regardless of the time of day.''

Solving Disputes

"There are some roads not to follow...and some ground which should not be contested."

（途有所不由。。。地有所不争。）

Sun Tze

Chinese culture places a premium on harmony. Open conflict is something to be avoided. When disputes arise in a contract, the Chinese prefer to resolve them through amicable, non-binding conciliation talks between the parties. While amicable dispute settlement will probably be frustrating, time-consuming, and not entirely amicable, it is still the preferable means.

In fact, most Chinese contracts contain a provision emphasising friendly negotiations, in the event that disputes arise between the parties. The Foreign Economic Contract Law stipulates in Article 37 that:

"In the case of a dispute, contracting parties will do everything possible to settle it through consultation or mediation by a third party."

If the parties do not want to settle their dispute through consultation or third-party mediation, or if the consultation or mediation fails, they may submit the case to Chinese or other arbitration bodies according to the contract terms or a written agreement reached on arbitration after the dispute.

One example of a dispute being settled without a fight involved one US multinational first negotiating with the Chinese partner, a shareholding company; then going to the shareholders themselves to exert pressure; then turning to the Ministry of Light Industry the administrative organ above the company; then going to what was then the State Council Production Office. As Sun Tze's son Sun Ping once advised General Tien Chi, "To unravel a knot you must not hold it tight. To settle a quarrel you must not join in the fighting. If we leave what is knotted and attack what is loose, making further entanglement impossible, matters can be sorted out."

Many contracts contain an arbitration clause designating arbitration in third countries in the event that friendly negotiations become less than friendly. The objective from the Chinese side is to avoid open confrontation, and (short of arbitration) keep the relationship going.

The Final Stages

> "*Nothing is more difficult than the art of manoeuvre. What is difficult about manoeuvre is trying to make the most devious route direct, and to turn misfortune into advantage.*"
> (凡用兵之法。。。莫难于军争。
> 军争之难者，以迂为直，以患为利。)
>
> Sun Tze

It is quite common for the Chinese to try to force reductions in the contract price in the last stages of discussion. Indeed, they will wait until the final touches are being put to negotiations — or at least appear to be. That is when they set the stage for driving an even harder bargain.

The Chinese know that once rumours of a concluded negotiation become public, the foreign firm will not be able to back down from the deal. For the foreign firm to renege on a publicised China deal would mean embarrassment and necessary explanations to both stockholders and corporate headquarters. In one case, the contract was signed with a closing banquet and all the accompanying fanfare. When the contract was sent for approval, the higher authorities refused to approve it. The terms were apparently not to their liking. For the foreign firm, reputation was on the line. The closing banquet had already been held, the

31

photographs had been taken, and the news spread back home. For the foreign firm, there was no pulling out.

One reason why the Chinese are not in a rush to make deals, according to some experts, is that they need to show their superiors what shrewd bargainers they are. "It won't make them feel good if you conclude the deal in the shortest time," said one China trader. "Go to see the Great Wall with them before beginning tough negotiations." Another tactic is to beef-up your draft contract with a lot of points which unnecessarily and excessively favour the foreign side. The Chinese negotiators can then cut these out through the course of tough negotiations, and then report back to their superiors that substantial gains have been made at the negotiation table with the foreign side.

Once negotiations are over and everyone is getting ready to sign the contracts, foreign businessmen should try not to look too happy. The danger in doing so is that they might give the Chinese reason to suspect that they have been outdone in the agreement. As Sun Tze wrote, "When capable, feign incapacity; when active, inactivity." In other words, smile but don't laugh.

Part IV

36 STRATEGIES

Strategy 1: Cross the Sea by Deceiving the Sky (瞒天过海)

Interpretation :   *To hide secrets in the obvious so as to avoid detection.*

Sometimes the most subtle trick is the most obvious. You don't want to question what seems obvious.

This strategy is rooted in China's Warring States Period. Some 2,000 years ago, China was divided into various different kingdoms which fought against each other. One kingdom was named Qin, another Chu.

A brilliant strategist named Baili Xi lived in the State of Chu. The king of Qin, hearing of his expertise, wanted Baili Xi as his advisor. The question was how to get him out of Chu without the king of Chu realising that Qin was gaining an advantage.

The trick employed was to accuse Baili Xi of being a fugitive from Qin. Of course the king of Chu did not want fugitives from Qin running around his kingdom, so he agreed that Qin soldiers could come and get their so-called fugitive. Of course it is not worth spilling blood over a fugitive. Qin soldiers then entered Chu, shackled Baili Xi and ignominiously dragged him across the kingdom and across the border into the kingdom of Qin.

The king of Chu thinking Baili Xi had no value, was relieved to see one less fugitive running around his kingdom. When Baili Xi reached the kingdom of Qin, the king received him, put him in fine silken robes, and made him a top advisor.

When negotiating in China, things may not always be what they seem. The subtle is never obvious. One should never take anything at its face value.

Sometimes western businessmen coming to China are impressed by what they see. For instance, one Chinese company received the western delegation at the airport, drove them to a construction site with many workers sitting around, and explained that this was where they were building a mega-project shopping mall and apartment complex.

Then they drove the party to see a field full of ducks and told them that this was their property, and they were going to build a whole satellite city "like Shatin in Hong Kong." The ducks ran away as the delegation walked through the muddy field.

Afterwards, they hosted a banquet attended by several city officials who all expressed support for anyone willing to invest in their city. (Everyone ate Peking duck as a main course.)

The foreign delegation went away impressed and convinced that they had the right Chinese partner with many impressive projects in a city where the officials supported both the Chinese party and the investment projects.

Little did the unwary foreign investors realise that the workers were sitting around the site because financing had stopped and construction could not continue; the duck-filled fields were up for grabs to whoever wanted to put up the cash to develop them; and the city officials would support anyone who came with a checkbook to invest anything in the city. In fact, the local officials saw the Chinese party as only a middleman facilitating western investment. (The ducks ran away when investors walked through the fields because they were afraid of being caught and served in Peking style.)

Strategy 2: Besiege Wei to Rescue Zhao (围魏救赵)

Interpretation :   To attack an adversary's weakest point (e.g. attack an adversary's lieutenant), divide and rule.

During the Warring States Period, the kingdom of Wei attacked the kingdom of Zhao, and surrounded Zhao by besieging its main fortress-city. Seeing his predicament, the king of Zhao sent for help from its ally, the kingdom of Qi.

Realising that Wei's forces were all deployed in full force around the kingdom of Zhao, the king of Qi thought that it would be better not to engage Wei head-on (in fact the king of Qi wanted to reserve his strength and not waste troops helping an ally — but at the same time he wanted to help his ally, otherwise if Zhao fell then Wei would be on his doorstep).

So he devised a stratagem. Qi did the unexpected. Qi sent its troops to besiege the capital of Wei, which had been left relatively undefended because all of Wei's troops were busy besieging Zhao. Wei had no choice but to call off the siege of Zhao and rushed back to protect its own capital from the Qi invaders!

When your adversary is busy doing something which is competitive against you, you can avoid fighting against him directly by attacking his vital parts which the adversary must do his best to rescue and protect.

This strategy was applied successfully when one large European company was negotiating a major industrial project with a Chinese party from Hubei Province in a hotel in Shenzhen. On the last day of negotiations, the parties were reaching a deadlock on a number of issues. When things really began to heat up, the Chinese party, to everybody's surprise (to be read as shock), announced that they had arranged lunch at a local Hubei-style restaurant nearby. The focus of the attack had been changed.

The Europeans insisted that they should continue with the negotiations especially as these were critical issues. The Chinese however, insisted that lunch had already been arranged (and paid for) and therefore everybody *must* move venue to the restaurant (and of course it was a Hubei restaurant so how could the European party refuse to eat the Chinese party's home cooking — which might be considered rude).

Lunch soon deteriorated into a Maotai *ganbei* contest with the Chinese party alternating among themselves in toasting the foreigners so as to get as many people on the foreign side as drunk as possible. In the middle of the banquet, the Chinese arranged a floor-show on the restaurant make-shift stage (usually used for Chinese weddings) where announcements were made that the joint venture would be established, to the surprise (to be read as shock) of the Europeans and in violation of the confidentiality agreement signed between both parties earlier.

Nevertheless, after a ten-course meal and uncountable rounds of Maotai, the foreign party found themselves back at the negotiation table in the afternoon humidity of Shenzhen, with no air-conditioning, but the windows of the room open to the noise and dust outside which flowed in to fill the room and the inebriated minds of the Europeans, trying to sort out their positions on the remaining key issues amidst burps and hiccups, (and the blur of a starch enriched and Maotai soaked lunch).

The Chinese party however, had carefully rotated its drinkers so as to reduce and limit the intake of its key negotiators, who remained fresh. "Shall we begin?" they asked. "I think we left off on this issue..."

Strategy 3: Kill with a Borrowed Knife (借刀杀人)

Interpretation :   To make use of someone else's resources to do your job.

During the Warring States Period, Fei Wuji, the Vice Premier of the kingdom of Chu was secretly jealous of the fact that the rising star warrior Xi Wan was favoured by none other than the Premier Nang Wa himself. In fact, Fei Wuji wanted to kill Xi Wan, but of course could not do this with his own hand.

One day, Xi Wan was excited because the Premier Nang Wa was going to pay a visit upon him. He expected to have great favours bestowed upon him. He therefore asked Fei Wuji to advise him what he should do to impress Nang Wa.

Fei Wuji in turn suggested that since Xi Wan's sword was famous throughout the land, he should present his sword to Nang Wa in the most solemn of occasions. Good idea, thought Xi Wan, who quickly arrayed his soldiers with full gear at strict attention on both sides of his reception room, and lay his polished sword before him to await Nang Wa's visit.

Meanwhile, Fei Wuji warned Nang Wa to take precautions when visiting Xi Wan, as he had heard a rumour that Xi Wan wanted to assassinate Nang Wa. Nang Wa brushed off the rumour and rode off to visit Xi Wan. When Nang Wa saw Xi Wan's troops in full combat gear waiting on each side of Xi Wan, who was poised with the polished sword drawn before him, Nang Wa thought it was a trap and ordered his troops to attack Xi Wan, who committed suicide in his grief. After that Nang Wa listened only to Fei Wuji, who he believed had saved his life. As a result, Fei Wuji became extremely powerful.

Mao Zedong's wife, Jiang Qing, used to love screaming, "I wish I had a knife in my hand" during momentary tantrums, in which everyone in the Diaoyutai State Guest House (which she had taken over as her own private quarters during the Cultural Revolution) would go to great extremes to appease her temper. Using the medium of "culture" during the Cultural Revolution, and the three stooges of Wang Hongwen, Zhang

Chunqiao, and Yao Wenyuan (who comprised the other three of the "Gang of Four") she wielded great power from the Diaoyutai State Guest House using other people to do the dirty work for her.

The strategy of "killing with a borrowed knife" involves using someone else's tool to achieve your own ends. Front companies established in Hong Kong with high-level political backers in China, who cannot soil their hands in business is a perfect example of this strategy successfully applied, especially when they have a Hong Kong tycoon who wants to polish his *guanxi* in China by footing the bill.

One Chinese developed the strategy of "killing with a borrowed knife" into a fine art. Mr Wang, a Hainanese, left China in 1989 (when the going wasn't so good) only to return to China in 1990 in possession of a foreign passport. Claiming to be a multimillionaire overseas Chinese prepared to invest vast sums into the motherland's reconstruction, he quickly obtained access to a number of senior leaders in China at a time when China was hungry for investors.

Following a number of photo sessions with a range of Chinese leaders which included the likes of Wan Li, Liu Huaqing, and the late Wang Zhen, Wang took his portfolio of photographs in hand, and went back overseas to demonstrate his vast network of *guanxi* in China and rounded up a few overseas Chinese who believed him and proceeded to make proceeds available to begin spending as seed money on infrastructure projects.

With a few properties under his belt and the sprouting of projects everywhere, Wang then dashed back to Hainan, his home base and demonstrated to the local officials and friends there that he was tied up with the power elite of the Central Government and had cash backers as well. A few real estate projects were made available to him and he purchased these plots of land and began to drop seed money on these projects (which involved mostly land speculation on Hainan's budding real estate boom).

Wang then began to court bigger foreign investors, showing both his pictures taken with China's power elite and the actual projects which were beginning to rise out of the dust of Haikou City in Hainan.

Impressed with this, the foreign investors decided to list Wang's company overseas, and began forking out money of their own to pay the underwriters, lawyers and merchant bankers. Now Wang with merchant bankers behind him (all thinking that they were buying into Wang's impressive *guanxi* network), Wang was seen as more impressive than ever in Hainan, with a namecard which listed more companies on it than the Hainan Yellow Pages.

Strategy 4: Relax and Wait for the Adversary to Tire Himself Out (以逸待劳)

Interpretation :   To use patience to wear down the adversary.

During the Warring States Period, when Pang Juan of the Kingdom of Wei went to attack the Kingdom of Qi, his archival, Sun Ping (the descendant of Master Sun Tze — who had had both legs cut off by Pang Juan during an earlier encounter) cautioned caution. "Don't rush into battle against these men. Just wait — take it easy" (interpretation from the classical Chinese text).

Instead of tiring out his own troops by rushing to the battlefield to meet Pang Juan halfway, Sun Ping chose to wait in a valley filled with cassia trees. He then arrayed his best archers on each side of the valley's steep walls and told them, "When you see a light in the valley, shoot!"

Sun Ping then wrote a message saying, "Under this tree, Pang Juan dies," and had it tacked onto a tree at the far end of the valley.

Pang Juan's troops meanwhile returned at full speed to rescue the capital of Wei from Qi's siege. Pang Juan ordered his tired troops to push on. Meanwhile, Sun Ping's troops relaxed in the valley waiting in ambush for Pang Juan's troops. The troops arrived at the valley only to find it empty and full of cassia trees.

Where were Sun Ping's troops? It was dark and nobody could see a thing in the valley. Sun Ping's troops who were hiding on each side behind the rocks listened as Pang Juan's troops clumsily pushed their way through the cassia trees. When Pang Juan found the note tacked to the tree, he lit a match to read the message. Upon seeing the light, Sun Ping's troops let their arrows fly into the valley.

" 按兵不动," is one of China's most ancient four character proverbs. It means "to hold the troops and not move."

Master Sun Tze counselled in his ancient text, "move only when it is to your advantage."

Wait and see tactics are frequently employed in Chinese negotiations with foreign investors who may be just a little too eager to do the deal.

This is what one American company discovered when they were negotiating their first joint venture. They sent one of the managers from their Taiwan office into China on the basic assumption that because he spoke mandarin, he would be able to negotiate the deal.

The Taiwan manager worked diligently, against a tight self-imposed time schedule. He put enormous pressure on himself, his team, and when everything was done properly and in full detail and against the time schedule, he arrived in China and found that the Chinese party would not sign. The contract in fact took all the power away from the old chairman of the factory under the new joint venture scheme being proposed. The chairman however, had little to say except that they could not sign the contract until clearer terms relating to production were included.

The foreign party went back to the drawing board and worked out a series of production schemes that would fulfil the requirement. Again, exhausting themselves against a self-imposed deadline, they arrived at the negotiating table in China only to hear that the contract could not be signed because there was not enough "hard equity" being put in.

The foreign party scrambled back to the drawing board and after re-doing the contract in a rush to meet their own deadlines, arrived in China only to hear the old factory chairman suggest that they speak to the local government officials responsible for approving the contract and hear their views. Being a small city, these local officials were of course, close friends of the chairman. The officials just nodded their heads as they listened to the explanations of the foreign party. They then concluded that some changes needed to be made, but were unclear what changes needed to be made or how many of these changes would have to be made before they would consider approving the agreement.

Against tight schedules to fulfil corporate goal-post measurement requirements, more changes were made which led to cutting major portions of the contract out including the controls over the old factory chairman. To everyone's surprise he signed and it was approved shortly thereafter.

Strategy 5: Loot a Burning House (趁火打劫)

Interpretation :   To exploit and capitalise on an opportunity at the expense of your adversary's chaotic situation.

During the Three Kingdoms Period, there was a standoff between Cao Cao and his enemies, Sun Quan and Zhou Yu. Cao Cao lost in battle when the others burned his ships after he was tricked into chaining them together. Cao Cao had no choice but to flee, leaving behind the territory which he had controlled in a state of chaos.

To everyone's surprise, a third rival Liu Bei and his master strategist Zhuge Liang led their troops and invaded the territory with ease (before Sun Quan and Zhou Yu realised what was happening) amidst the chaos, and made the most of the pickings which Cao Cao had left behind.

This is a strategy the British are learning from the Chinese after many years of negotiating, and the realisation that a nearly bankrupt country such as the United Kingdom has few real bargaining chips against the world's next economic super-power.

For instance, Hong Kong's Government has been generating much publicity by drawing attention to the democratic future of Hong Kong, when in fact Hong Kong has never had democracy historically throughout 100 years of British colonial rule.

Of course what many people feel is that the British Government really wants to create a degree of chaos in Hong Kong to draw international attention away from the feeling that the main intention of the British colonialists is to create as many pretexts for draining off Hong Kong's foreign exchange reserves (as was done in other British colonies in the past).

Some cynics feel that one of the key tactics being employed to strip Hong Kong of its foreign exchange reserves is Britain's insistence upon building a white-elephant airport which will result in the dishing out of fat construction and consulting contracts to British companies without much competitive bidding. This airport will involve huge land reclamations by filling the sea alongside Lantau Island and also involve the creation of vast tracts of land through the reclamation of most of Hong Kong's harbour, to be sold off to speculative local investors before 1997. As all this land will technically be under "Crown Lease" until 1997, everyone can be sure into whose coffers the cash will flow.

Strategy 6: Make a Feint to the East While Attacking in the West (声东击西)

Interpretation : To confuse your adversary's command, and mislead your adversary.

Between the end of the Qin Dynasty and the beginning of the Han, Xiang Yu and Liu Bang fought between each other to see who would succeed as emperor. However, in the beginning they were friends. One day, Liu Bang wanted to leave Xiang Yu's side to go off to another territory using as an excuse, his desire to fetch his parents back. Xiang Yu was afraid that Liu Bang might run off and set himself up elsewhere in a rival kingdom. Being clever, Xiang Yu insisted instead that he send his own men to fetch Liu Bang's parents and keep them as hostage, in the meantime letting Liu Bang set off on whatever venture he wanted to pursue.

This strategy is applied to situations where one says (or does) one thing on one hand to mislead others, while their real intention is to do something completely different.

Mao Zedong applied this strategy over and over again in his battles against the Kuomintang. In fact at Chi Shui (Red River), Mao crossed the river no less than four times. Each time, when Chiang Kaishek expected him not to cross, he would cross. Then when Chiang sent troops to the other side to fight the Red Army, Mao ordered his men to cross back. This strategy completely confused Chiang and allowed Mao to get enough breathing space to move his troops to eventual safety.

Pretending to move in one direction while actually moving in the other is probably the most basic and fundamental negotiation tool which can be applied in either diplomatic or business negotiations (as if there is a difference between the two).

At the time of this writing, China-US trade relations are dominated by ongoing negotiations over the US trade deficit with China. As China's economic growth reels into an export promotion cycle, the US is faced with entrenched unions, brass industries, and a society which is just too comfortable with the status quo to be competitive against China on the export front. (What the US economy needs is not another invasion of a small caribbean island to bolster nationalism at home, but a complete revitalisation and reorientation of her domestic industry.) The problem is that while this revitalisation is being debated in all the committees of Congress, the US wants to keep as many Chinese goods off its domestic markets as it can, and try to force open the Chinese market to US goods.

While this is the fact, obviously US trade negotiators cannot come out and say this directly, otherwise they would not even have a leg to stand (or sit) on at the negotiation table. The solution to the negotiation strategy has therefore been to "make a feint to the east while attacking from the west."

While the real issue is the US trade deficit, the issues on the negotiation table are: protection of US intellectual property rights in China and human rights. The US doesn't seem concerned with intellectual property or human rights in other places such as Taiwan and South Korea (where both are flagrantly abused), but is very concerned with these problems when negotiating with China.

While counterfeit CDs can be purchased in just about any open market in South Korea, Taiwan, Hong Kong, Singapore, Thailand, Malaysia, and India, the US trade negotiators in 1995 demanded that China close down eleven factories allegedly producing counterfeit CDs. This demand was made to the Ministry of Foreign Trade and Economic Cooperation, which is neither the organ in China responsible for protecting intellectual property, nor the body responsible for State enterprises.

Obviously, the demands could not be met as presented by the US negotiation team. Therefore, this situation can be used as a justification for the US to slap sanctions on Chinese imports. While putting one set of demands on the table and insisting on demands that could not reasonably be met, the US negotiators have created an excuse to achieve their real objective of restricting Chinese imports to help sort out the US trade deficit problem.

Strategy 7: Create Something Out of Nothing
(无中生有)

Interpretation : Turn something that was not substantial into reality.

During the Qin Dynasty, there were two rebels, Chen Sheng and Wu Guang, who wanted to overthrow the Qin Emperor. However, both men faced the problem that they did not have enough supporters between them in order to carry out a successful revolt against the Qin Emperor. In order to build up the supporters which they lacked, they placed letters in the stomachs of fish saying that "Chen Sheng will become the Emperor" and released the fish into a stream.

As the fishermen along both sides of the stream began to catch these fish and cut open their stomachs, they found the messages. A rumour soon spread among the people that Chen Sheng was destined to become the Emperor. As a result, momentum was built to support Chen Sheng in his revolt against the Qin Emperor, and waves of volunteers began to stream into the ranks of his fledgling army.

This strategy involves creating momentum out of nothing in order to bring about something real.

In 1988, when the Central Government decided that Hainan Island (then one of the most underdeveloped regions in China and a part of Guangdong Province) should become an independent province and Special Economic Zone, an unbelievable amount of publicity was focused on building up Hainan to be the future centre of commercial opportunity in China. In fact, in those days Hainan was being regarded as the "next Hong Kong" and because of its deserted sandy beaches, as the "Hawaii of China" (two development concepts which are diametrically opposite).

The propaganda which surrounded the development of Hainan Province into a province and Special Economic Zone was so great that even the Chinese believed it themselves. University graduates from all over China flooded into Hainan seeking jobs which did not exist.

There was an elaborate plan to develop Hainan into an area having a special technology zone, manufacturing, tourism, and industrial zones. Between 1988 and 1990, floods of businessmen went to Hainan to find that local nepotism among other factors made a straightforward business deal (if there is one in China) difficult if not impossible.

Nevertheless, the explosion of excitement about Hainan led to such an influx of traders and businessmen on the back of hopes that Hainan would be a grand experiment in economic reform. The result of this gold rush was that Hainan became a centre of speculation, entertainment, and a number of vices which spell big business, but which are exactly what the Central Government leaders wanted to keep out of China (being the reason why they designated Hainan — an island, to be the target for such experimentation). The result was that Hainan grew and prospered. The graduates landed good-paying jobs.

"Creating something out of nothing" is a tactic regularly employed by foreign investors as well in trying to get approval for their investments in China. "Technology transfer" rings bells in the minds of officials seeking to achieve policy objectives related to developing an export promotion economy on the back of a programme of technology import substitution.

Projects are therefore often approved on the hot air that great technology will be transferred to China and the skill levels of the Chinese people will be raised through the transfer of such technology (which if actually believed would have one thinking that all investors were Peace Corps volunteers in razor sharp suits toting briefcases of goodwill).

"We really care about the people," is a favourite line thrown upon tried and dull ears of officials receiving visitor after visitor. Talks of great commitment without cash is one factor which drove the State Council in 1988 to promulgate regulations requiring foreign investors to put up at least fifteen percent of their registered capital within three months of obtaining a business licence to invest (or lose the licence) so as to prevent big talkers from creating nothing out of nothing.

Strategy 8: Pretend to Advance Down One Path While Taking Another Hidden Path (暗度陈仓)

Interpretation : *To distract the enemy by making a deliberate gesture to attack in one direction while attacking in another where the enemy does not defend.*

This strategy dates back to the Han Dynasty when the legendary strategist Liu Bang wanted to attack his adversary Xiang Yu. In order to implement this attack, Liu Bang ordered some of his troops to cut a wide road so as to clear a passage in the forest for their troops to march forward and carry out a direct attack against Xiang Yu. This however, was only a ploy to draw the attention of Xiang Yu away from Liu Bang's real intention.

While a group of Liu Bang's troops were making noise hacking a path through the forest, Liu Bang sent his real crack troops down a secret path to advance against Xiang Yu's flank without him being aware that the larger troop movement was taking place. When Liu Bang's troops finally attacked Xiang Yu, he was unprepared having been busy making preparations against the small troop cutting the road through the forest, and was taken by complete surprise.

This strategy involves a sleight of hand, that is doing one thing in the open while really making another unsuspected real move. Let's see how foreign multinationals can apply this stratagem in opening up the China market.

China knows that foreign investors have been hungry for opportunities to enter the China market of 1.3 billion. There was a day when foreigners thought that they could sell one shoe lace to every Chinese, and fortunes could be made on the back of the country's population statistics. Consequently, today most international companies have only one thought in mind — selling to China. The question is how best to do that in a market where approvals are still required for many activities and certain imports are highly restricted.

Many multinationals simply want to sell their products to China. China wants them to manufacture and also to have foreign companies invest in the country, to enable China to obtain the technology, skills, and the productive capabilities of its western trade partners (and future economic competitors).

Consequently, in order to increase chances for survival in the budding market, western suppliers have finally begun to realise that market entry can only be attained by establishing joint ventures. Some of these do not even involve the transfer of much technology, but rather the establishment of minimum value-added manufacturing, to allow these companies to get their products into the market. "If you want to be there for the long-term, you have to manufacture in the country," said one high-powered executive with an American multinational.

Take one US multinational whose only interest was selling its product in the China market, and cracking the retail sector (a sensitive area at the time of this writing). It couldn't establish a retail joint venture, so instead it developed a "manufacturing" venture in a small town, using the minimum investment and least technology.

Essentially, the venture was a minor value-added assembly centre, used as a base for getting products around the country. While claiming that this was to be its first joint venture to begin product manufacturing through a programme of technology transfer, it in fact was only a bogus manufacturing operation and really a product distribution centre.

Strategy 9: Watch the Fire Burning from Across the River (隔岸观火)

Interpretation : To allow your adversaries to fight the enemy themselves while you rest and observe, and later defeat the exhausted survivor.

During the Three Kingdoms Period, Generals Yuan Xiang and Yuan Xi led armies from each of the two of the Three Kingdoms which were warring among themselves. Cao Cao who led the army of the third kingdom however, did not lead his troops against either Yuan Xiang or Yuan Xi. Instead he held back his troops and sat on the sidelines waiting for both sides to annihilate themselves before stepping in.

When in negotiations, watch the situation carefully. If there is any hint of discord or internal conflict among the opposite party, then this in itself offers an opportunity. Bidding one's time and waiting, one can allow internal conflicts to bring the opposite party to the position which one wants.

The strategy of "watching the fire burning from across the river" involves patiently waiting for your opponent to have splits in its own ranks.

China applies this strategy every year during the annual US-China trade negotiations. The US Commerce Department's negotiators shake their fingers at China and accuse it of intellectual property and human rights violations, when the real issue at stake is the US Government's own trade deficit with China. "If China doesn't do this ... and doesn't do that ...," the Commerce Department negotiators scream, "then we will teach China a lesson by slapping tariffs on these goods ... and those goods ..."

The Chinese Government then sends out subtle (and sometimes not so subtle) hints to those big US corporations manufacturing and seeking to manufacture in China (who are responsible for footing the campaign dollars which get US presidents elected), that such actions by the US

Government may be reciprocated by similar (yet different!!!) action in China. Alarm bells ring.

American Chamber of Commerce representatives from Hong Kong, Shanghai and Beijing send their lobbying teams to Washington insisting that the US negotiators stop their threats. When one US Secretary of Commerce, Christopher Warren dropped the tariff threat in Beijing, China's Minister of Foreign Affairs, Qian Jiqian simply explained that if the US wanted to put tariffs on Chinese shoes being sold to the US, then China would stop selling shoes to the US altogether. Qian made his point by emphasising that the Secretary of Commerce could explain the situation to America's consumers as well as retailers and the shoe industry as a whole when he went back.

In such cases, the US negotiators have to cope with divisions on their homefront, the US Government and the US business groups which constitute the ultimate constituency of the US Government. As the internal squabbling heats up, the pressure on China cools down, and the issues get kicked back another year, for another day of negotiation — at least.

Strategy 10: Conceal a Dagger in a Smile (笑里藏刀)

Interpretation : To make your adversary relax and unaware of your enmity, hide hostility under friendliness.

During the Tang Dynasty, the Emperor Tang Gao Zhong had a high ranking minister named Li Yi Fu who was influential at the Tang court. Li Yi Fu was known for smiling and being conciliatory to anyone who was his superior while at the same time hating them inside.

The Emperor did not realise that Li Yi Fu was such a black-hearted individual as Li Yi Fu was always showering praises on the Emperor and grinning with smiles. The Emperor ignored the warnings of others about Li, believing only in Li's sincerity as gleaned from his smile.

In Cantonese, people like this are referred to as "Smiling Tigers" (笑面虎).

Very often, one will see this situation in the internal relations of their Chinese counterpart. The Chairman or General Manager of a Chinese factory may really carry the respect of his workers, but at the same time will have sycophants fawning over him, lighting his cigarettes, pouring his tea, and heaping praises on their leader to the point where he himself never knows who his real friends or supporters are.

Others simply like the fawning and believe the words of the syco-phants.

This however, is not only limited to Chinese corporate structure set-ups, but is probably a problem for the readers of this book as well. Just look around the office and see who fawns the most !

The famous Tang Dynasty poet, Bai Juyi wrote, "The likes of Li Yi Fu are always smiling, and a dagger hides behind the smiles."

Strategy 11: Sacrifice the Plum for the Peach
(李代桃僵)

Interpretation : If need be, sacrifice the less important in order to preserve the vital; substitute one thing for another.

During the Warring States Period, a high-ranking district leader Wei Xun Cong named his son Ji Ze to become his successor. He arranged an engagement for his son with Xun Zhen, the daughter of one of the leaders of the State of Chi. But upon seeing the beauty of the girl, the father decided that he wanted the girl for himself, and banned his son to another region to get him out of the way.

The girl later had two sons of her own, one named So and the other named Suo. The father liked the two new children and rejected his older son. The new young wife suggested that Ji Ze, the banned eldest son and designated successor, be killed. However, one of her two sons was actually closer to Ji Ze, his half-brother, than to his own full-brother. In order to save Ji Ze, the youngest son So wore Ji Ze's clothes and was assassinated by his mother's henchmen as a result.

The moral of the story is to give away one precious thing in order to get another. The end result is not always what is expected however.

Just as in imperial dynastic succession, in equity joint ventures, control is the single most important issue for both the Chinese as well as foreign parties.

The China-Foreign Equity Joint Venture Law when adopted in 1979 required the Chinese party to always be the Chairman of joint ventures. Amendments to the law in 1990 relaxed this position, allowing the Chairman to be appointed by either party, subject to agreement between the two.

Under Chinese law, the Chairman of the joint venture is the "legal representative." His signature can bind the joint venture.

For the Chinese party, this position is important as the Chairman of a factory is often an old time cadre having spent most of his life with the

54

enterprise and carries the respect and weight of responsibility of both the enterprise and the community to which that enterprise is attached.

For the foreign party, they are concerned about legal liability and the dangers of what a legal representative might do after kicking back too many Maotai's or XO's in the karaoke bar.

Control is a critical issue for the foreign party as well. Control means the maintenance of the products being produced by the joint venture. Without management control, foreign investors are reluctant to put their cash on the table.

For the Chinese party, control means face and power. For the foreign party, it means quality control and profitability.

The compromise is often an inside deal, with the foreign party giving the Chairmanship position away to the Chinese party in exchange for the position of the General Manager of the joint venture. Contracts will be drawn up separating management from the Board of Directors, giving the General Manager extensive control and supervision over the operations of the joint venture, with the Board of Directors limiting its decision-making to broad policy and directional issues.

The Chairman of the Board may then have its power limited to only being able to sign on behalf of the joint venture or execute decisions which have been made by a vote of the Board, thereby making any independent action by the Chairman invalid.

The General Manager in turn will take control of the actual quality and operational issues of the joint venture. In this way, in negotiations one is often able to sacrifice the plum position of visible power in order to preserve vital control on the inside.

Strategy 12: Take Away a Goat in Passing (顺手牵羊)

Interpretation : To capitalise on your adversary's negligence or incompetence when the choice is right.

During the early Ming Dynasty, Emperor Zhu Di came to power by kicking out his predecessor Jian Wen Di, who was said to have run away and hid somewhere in the jungles of Southeast Asia. Emperor Zhu Di commanded that Jian Wen Di be found and brought back. His famous eunuch-general Zheng He, upon hearing this command took a big navy with him and sailed off looking for Jian Wen Di.

While Zheng He never really found Jian Wen Di, he had a great time overseas, using the emperor's navy to conquer other nations in Southeast Asia. The result was he didn't do what he was supposed to, but instead had a great time getting away with a lot else.

This strategy has since come to apply to situations where one is able to get away with much more than they expected.

Taking away a goat from the enemy as it passes by is easy to do, especially when the enemy is in a rush.

Negligence characterises the way a number of western companies try to negotiate deals in China. The euphoria of doing the China deal, and the rush to jump into the market headlong, leaves room for lots of mistakes.

As one executive explained, "Don't let your chief executive officer fly in, get enchanted and make a promise that will later handcuff your negotiation. The Chinese love it when they know a company's negotiator is under pressure from the boss to close the deal."

When one American multinational was anxious to manufacture their product in Guangzhou, they linked up with a Hong Kong group which claimed to have family contacts in one of the small cities in Guangdong. The foreign party never investigated the truth of these contacts independently. They believed the Hong Kong group's claims at their face value, and soon found themselves hamstrung having given away their key negotiating position — the fact that they were very anxious to begin production as soon as possible so as to meet scheduled orders.

The Chinese party went ahead and presented them with the contract and related documents, the terms of which are completely unacceptable. The Hong Kong group acting as negotiators had already given away most of their negotiation ability on the fact that everyone knew that the foreign party had already committed to a production schedule to begin within a six-week period after the contracts had been presented by the Chinese party.

When the foreign investors complained to the Chinese party and their Hong Kong partners, the simple answer was that, "If you don't sign on the documents in the form that they are in, it will take longer to approve the project and we know that you are anxious to begin production."

Similarly, the author of this book cannot even count the number of times that foreign businessmen have returned from the negotiating table with signed letters of intent or contracts without fully digesting the meaning of what they had signed. In many instances, they have even entered into agreements drafted in Chinese without understanding what is written in the agreement!

"But we really trust the Chinese party because we have such a good relationship with them. They took us to so many banquets, and refused to let us pay for anything," explained one western businessmen who brought his letter of intent signed in Chinese for translation.

Strategy 13: Beat the Grass to Startle the Snake
(打草惊蛇)

Interpretation : Do not tip off your adversary.

During the Warring States Period, the king of Zhongshan had two gorgeous courtesans named Yinji and Jiangji. Each wanted to rise to be the king's queen in her own right. Yinji however, had a famous strategist as a friend who agreed to help her. The strategist advised the king that his neighbour, the king of Zhao, wanted to take Yinji away and have her for his own.

The king of Zhongshan was terribly upset and did not know what to do because he realised that while he wanted to keep Yinji for his own, he did not have enough troops to defeat the kingdom of Zhao in war if push came to shove. The strategist however, had an idea. Certainly if the king of Zhongshan raised Yinji to the level of queen, then even the king of Zhao would not want to pick an unnecessary fight.

While in those days it was one thing to crave and even demand another's courtesan, it was considered not in good standing to want their queen. Consequently, Yinji became queen, and the king happily believed that by doing this, he would be able to keep Yinji.

In the old days, this strategy meant basically flushing out the enemy's position to get what one wants in the end. Today it has come to mean not tipping off one's adversary.

Sometimes in China, this strategy does not work out quite as the strategist planned, such as the instance when a Swedish negotiating team on a major telecommunications joint venture was negotiating with one of the foremost electronics companies from Nanjing in a Beijing hotel for about a week.

On the first day of the negotiation, the Swedish team kept their lawyer in the backroom to provide advice behind the scenes as they negotiated with the Chinese party over the joint venture contract.

On the second day of the negotiation, the Swedish team debated whether or not they should bring the lawyer into the room to negotiate directly with the Chinese party. They thought the Chinese party did not have a lawyer of their own and would therefore be at a disadvantage not realising that the foreign party had their lawyer present in the backroom throughout the negotiation.

On the third day of the negotiations, the Swedish team, bursting with confidence that the Chinese party was at a disadvantage because they did not have a lawyer, brought their lawyer to the table to toughen up the negotiation. The lawyer negotiated with the Chinese team over the contracts throughout the third and fourth day.

On the fifth day of the negotiations, when the Swedish team arrived in the room with their lawyer worn out by two days of negotiations, the Chinese lawyer was sitting next to the General Manager with the Chinese team primed and ready to hit the negotiation table hard. To the surprise of the Swedish team, the Chinese had brought their own lawyer along from Nanjing for the negotiations and he had been advising them from behind the scenes from his hotel room all along throughout the negotiation during the previous four days.

Strategy 14: Raise a Corpse from the Dead (借尸还魂)

Interpretation : To use something dead to achieve your own ends.

Of the "Eight Spirits" of Chinese mythology, Tie Guai Li was once a handsome man whose spirit decided to leave his body and fly around for about seven days to explore the other dimension. Before flying off from his handsome body, the spirit told the others to standby and wait for him as he would be back in seven days.

The others however, got tired of waiting and cremated the body. When Tie Guai Li's spirit flew back from the other dimension to this world seven days later, he went crazy because he could not find his old body which was now in ashes. Without any other choices available, he had to take the first body which was unoccupied by any soul, and flew into the body of a beggar who had just died. Ever since, Tie Guai Li has been depicted as an ugly beggar.

The Chinese government itself has adopted the strategy of "raising a corpse from the dead" in solving its own problem with revitalising defunct State-owned enterprises.

Today, China is facing a big problem with its State-owned enterprises. During the 1950s, under the influence of Soviet State planning, these enterprises were established, not to be commercially viable but to basically give people jobs and a reason for receiving an allocation of income. Efficiency was poor and the overall economic results worse.

Through a series of policy measures, State planning became reduced and these enterprises have had to adjust to the growing market sector of China's economy. This has meant that alot of these enterprises in a new market economy have no commercial basis to continue operation. With the acceptance of the bankruptcy concept over recent years in China, a number of State-owned factories have become vacant shells.

How to "raise a corpse from the dead"? China has begun an ambitious programme of experimentation with transforming State-owned enterprises into shareholding companies. Many of these shareholding companies are then selected for listing purposes on either of China's own domestic stock exchanges in Shanghai and Shenzhen. Virtually every State-owned enterprise in China is now looking to transform into a shareholding company and find a path to a listing. Where the betting is good, some enterprises are even selected for listings overseas in Hong Kong or even New York City.

Likewise, China's policy of encouraging foreign investment through joint ventures involving the transfer of foreign technology and management skills on the back of capital injections is another means of injecting new life into old corpses. State-owned enterprises which are notorious for inefficiency and low quality standards benefit from such transfers. Joint ventures are often signed for fixed time periods at the end of which the Chinese State-owned enterprise walks away not only with the capital injected but with the benefits of training, technical and management input over the course of the investment period.

Strategy 15: Lure the Tiger out of the Mountain (调虎离山)

Interpretation : To have your adversaries deploy their strongest element away from their defence base.

At the end of the Zhou Dynasty, the king of Zheng wanted to get rid of his younger brother because the latter wanted to become the king himself. The king had a strategy and told his brother that he himself was going to see the Emperor of Zhou. When the king left his capital, the younger brother followed the king with troops. In fact, the king did not go to see the Emperor at all but laid a trap along the roadside.

The younger brother led his own troops out of his own fiefdom, leaving the fiefdom unattended. The king in a smart pincer move attacked the brother's troops as they followed along the road, and at the same time moved into the younger brother's vacated fiefdom with his own troops.

Chairman Mao liked "luring the tiger out of the mountain." This is probably because he considered himself a tiger in a mountain that others could not lure.

Mao called the Americans "paper tigers" (纸老虎). After years of collapsed Sino-US relations, Mao was to first lure Kissinger, and then Nixon out of the mountain of America to China. Mao only left China to meet with a head of State once in his life, and that was to the Soviet Union. He never went again.

When Kissinger and Nixon finally made it to China, they never knew when they were to see Mao, until he summoned them. Kissinger and Nixon were resting at the Diaoyutai State Guest House. There was suddenly a stir of excitement at the Diaoyutai State Guest House, Hongqi limousines chugged through the gates, and Kissinger and Nixon were informed that Mao wanted to see them "at once" (which meant "now"). They were then whisked off to Mao's private library villa in Zhongnanhai, where he received them, in his own tiger's den.

When negotiating on the adversary's turf, one will always be at a disadvantage. Therefore, it is critical to find a way to "lure the tiger out of his own mountain" to put negotiations on an even playing field.

One German company is well-experienced in sending teams to a small city in central Hubei Province to negotiate with a factory. As the factory was one of the biggest local revenue generators, the factory ran the town. When teams went to negotiate, they stayed at the hotel which the factory arranged, and met when the factory managers wanted to meet them. The factory fixed the time of all meals (which were eaten in either the factory's canteen or in the restaurant owned by the factory). Every night, the negotiators were taken to the karaoke bar and discotheque owned by the factory. Days and weeks passed without any concrete results.

Finally the German team began to insist that negotiations be carried out in Beijing. They insisted on booking a conference room at one of the five-star hotels. They even agreed to help the factory managers pay for their rooms — anything to get them out of their home territory, and move negotiations onto neutral ground.

The factory managers finally came to Beijing where the German company could control the schedule more. Negotiations started every day with German punctuality at 8:30, and broke at lunch time. Negotiations then resumed again at 2:00 and ended at 7:00. Progress was made every day as the Germans set goals for each day's discussions — a situation which could never have been achieved if negotiations were conducted on the home territory of the Chinese party.

Strategy 16: Let the Adversary off in order to Snare Him (欲擒故纵)

Interpretation : Do not arouse your adversary's spirit to fight back.

At the beginning of the Han Dynasty, there was a king from Donghu who was a really arrogant man. He demanded that the king of Hun give him his fastest horse. Against the will of his advisors, the king of Hun agreed. The king of Donghu thinking even more of himself, demanded that the king of Hun give him his own wife. The king of Hun's advisors were furious and counselled against such conciliation. The king of Hun however, was especially clever and said, "No problem. If he wants my wife, he can have my wife", and turned the good lady over.

Thereafter, the king of Donghu looked down upon the king of Hun as useless and weak. In fact, the king of Donghu did not even bother reinforcing the defenses along the border with Hun, as he felt that the king of Hun was a coward. In fact, one day the king of Donghu, feeling proud and conceited, demanded that the king of Hun give him some land along their mutual border. To the surprise of his advisors the king of Hun said, "That's enough", and led his army across the undefended border to conquer all of the kingdom of Donghu.

"There are some rules not to follow ... and some ground which should not be contested" wrote Sun Tze some 2,000 years ago. Sun Tze was an advocate of never backing the enemy into a corner. In his treatise on the *Art of War*, Sun Tze recommended not to fight the enemy who had a river to its back with no escape. Better to let them think there are some escapes and then attack.

Western businessmen coming to China often hammer the issues too hard, and then complain that entering the China market is like trying to crack the Great Wall. Frustration is common amongst the foreign investors trying to negotiate complex contracts in China. The first lesson is not to show your frustration. The second is not to let the other party realise that you are actually frustrated with them.

It is critical that when negotiations reach an impasse to allow the Chinese party a way out. Sometimes this can be done by creating two optional scenarios, putting them forward on the negotiation table, and letting the Chinese party choose one. This will get better results than the foreign party trying to force its position on the Chinese party.

Similarly, it is important to always give the Chinese party "face". Even in a situation where there is an impasse, one should not vent their frustration. Once harsh words are thrown across the negotiation table, or the Chinese party feels boxed in the corner over a single issue, they will become entrenched on that issue, and weeks (sometimes months) can be thrown to the wind simply trying to resolve something which could have been avoided by simply giving the Chinese party some options to consider, or several alternative positions to choose from.

Strategy 17: Cast a Brick to Attract a Jade (抛砖引玉)

Interpretation : To use a bait (look alike) to catch something big.

During the Tang Dynasty, the Emperor Tang Taizhong wanted to possess a famous calligraphy work by the legendary calligrapher Wang Xizhi, from a monk who kept the calligraphy carefully guarded. So Tang Taizhong used a ploy by having a minister bring another of Wang Xizhi's works to the monk for comparison with the calligraphy held by the monk.

After comparing, the minister told the monk that the monk's calligraphy piece was a fake and not Wang Xizhi's real work. The monk disheartened, left the real calligraphy lying around unguarded, and went off to do something else. The minister seized the opportunity to steal the real calligraphy and run with it.

This is the tactic often employed by Hong Kong tycoons in trying to crack open the China market for themselves. They will make donations and contributions to various causes in China without blinking an eye or asking for anything in return for a period of time. Then when least expected, they will move in and demand certain conditions for their investments. The officials who have been on the receiving side for so long, have allowed themselves to be brought under an obligation, both real and psychological. The rest is a pure hijacking.

Take Hong Kong's most famous and favourite home-bred tycoon, Li Kai Shing. For years, Li Kai Shing refused to invest anything in China. Virtually all of his investment activities were in Hong Kong and later Canada, but never in China. Nevertheless, it was always there at the back of his mind.

His first step was to make donations. He donated schools mostly. A donation here, a donation there, all in the name of goodwill, always sowing seeds of goodwill (and with it an intrinsic obligation) wherever he went. Hungry hands forget today what may be asked of them tomorrow.

His second step was to express goodwill on the political front. When many Hong Kong tycoons were busy shooting their mouths off against China in 1989 following the events of 4 June, not a sound was heard from Li. When the Chinese economy turned full circle and began booming in the 1990s, and those same businessmen who ranted and raved at China in the summer of 1989 began to scuttle back kowtow kissing for business opportunities and handouts, Li was already there standing firm in a position of respect and goodwill. He then began to coordinate with the Chinese authorities on matters relating to the transfer of Hong Kong back to China in 1997. His credentials were credible.

In 1994, he decided it was time to cash in his goodwill chips. He asked for his big concession, a huge tract of land in central Beijing fronting the famous Chang An Avenue and Wangfujing, Beijing's 5th Avenue. The Beijing Municipal Government gave it to him — the whole thing — all except the most valuable tract, being the corner across from the famous Beijing Hotel occupied by American fastfood chain, McDonald's.

Li Kai Shing insisted on having things his own way. Having donated so much to China, and having invested in so many relations without asking for anything in return, it was time for him to fetch back a jade after having thrown in so many bricks. "If I can't have the corner I won't invest at all in China!" he allegedly told the Beijing Municipal authorities. "McDonald's will just have to go."

And so the authorities told McDonald's that their twenty-year contract would require some minor adjustments, mainly that they would have to move their largest retail operation in the world from its strategically important location. Despite the international commercial outrage at this incident, Li Kai Shing insisted, calling upon all the goodwill which he had demonstrated over the years while asking for nothing, to now ask for and get what most would have thought impossible.

Strategy 18: To Catch Bandits, Nab Their Ringleader First (擒賊先擒王)

Interpretation : Shoot at the horse first in order to shoot the rider.

During the Three Kingdoms period, Cao Cao was very smart and used Emperor Han Xian Di to tell everyone else what to do. Everytime Cao Cao wanted to do something, he had the Emperor do it for him and with the Emperor's edict, nobody dared challenge Cao Cao.

One should never underestimate the importance and extent of inter-personal networking *guanxi* which goes behind the patron-client relationships in China which makes the decision-making power of certain leaders at times appear to be all powerful.

One should realise however, that leaders always have their leaders and the chain of command eventually leads somewhere. This creates a situation where the powerful appear to be all powerful, and if one can obtain a decision (regardless of how oblique that decision is) from the top cadre on the totem-pole, then everyone beneath will fall in place — more or less at least that's the way the system is supposed to work.

Mao Zedong's leadership role fully illustrates the complexity of patron-client power relations in China. As unquestioned leader of the People's Republic after liberation, he obtained an almost untouchable and unreal statue, whereby words uttered from his mouth (taken in one context or another) could be used to give an unlimited authority to a certain event (like the Cultural Revolution), when left to those participants in the political in-fighting below to guess what the real meaning of Mao's words were, and to see who would come out on top when final interpretation would be made.

Today (at least at the time of the writing of this book), Deng Xiao Ping holds a similar statue in post-liberation China. Although Deng has resigned from all official posts, given his years in China's military, party, and political bureaucracies, and given the number of interlocking patron-client relations which eventually linked up, connecting to one leader, Deng is in a position to persuade and influence events simply by uttering general principals of direction within which the political strugglers beneath must work.

Similarly, among some Chinese State-owned enterprises, the chairman or director of the enterprise, if he has his political base and patron-client relations in place for enough years, may very well hold strict command over the decisions of that enterprise. In some cases in China, particularly in rural areas where a large enterprise may actually constitute the community as a whole, the chairman of the enterprise may be a "Tu Huang Di" ("dirt" or local emperor).

Chairman Teng was just such a dirt emperor, commanding an industrial chemical enterprise of some 1,500 people which constituted the entire city of what in fact was a small town of Hubei Province in central China. What Teng said about the enterprise's operations was law.

When a major European multinational began negotiations with the chemical factory for a joint venture, it was Teng's lieutenants who met with the European negotiating team for round after round of negotiations. The negotiations dragged on slowly like a barge clipping down the Yangtze River, without any apparent resolution on any of the key points.

Lack of resolution was further complicated by some internal political jockeying among the several lieutenants who constituted the Chinese party's core negotiating team. Some of the key managers were related to Teng while others served longer under him than their comrades. Chairman Teng meanwhile sat back at the factory headquarters in an overstuffed leather chair and either commanded the negotiations from behind the scenes taking in reports from his lieutenant managers or simply pitting one of his managers against another.

Realising that endless deadlocks would pervade in a situation such as this, the foreign team organized its negotiations in a nearby major city which was to be attended by the entire management team of the Chinese party and the entire European negotiating team consisting of financial specialists and technical personnel. When all management personnel of both sides were conveniently locked into negotiations on the top floor of a four-star hotel, the Managing Director of the foreign party along with one of the authors of this book got into a car and drove ahead across the province to the factory especially to meet with Chairman Teng privately for discussions.

One by one, the issues were flashed out on the table, and Teng's basic concerns were put forward. Teng, realising that he had not been receiving the full picture of the foreign party's concerns from his lieutenant managers, picked up a mobile phone and telephoned his financial manager during the middle of negotiations and uttered commands of exactly what he should say and do.

The Managing Director of the European party, then turned around and drove back across the province, arriving at the four-star hotel the next day in time for lunch and the last round of negotiations during which main points were finalised as had been pre-decided by Chairman Teng himself the day before.

As the old Chinese saying goes, "when the emperor says 'die', the people do not dare but to die" (君要臣死, 臣不得不死). Therefore, if you want to get the job done, sometimes it is easier to get the boss to do it for you.

Strategy 19: Remove the Fire from under the Cauldron
(釜底抽薪)

Interpretation : To wear down your adversary's resources first before attacking him; get at the root, take radical measures, effect a permanent cure.

During the Song Dynasty, Wu Zhu of the Jin kingdom wanted to conquer the Song. However, the Song were led by a famous marshal named Yue Fei who seemed invincible. Wu Zhu knew that he could not defeat Song unless he first got rid of Yue Fei. He did this by arranging the assassination of Yue Fei through counter-espionage before attacking.

For western businessmen, a negotiation in China may seem like a protracted guerilla warfare. This is because the Chinese are aware that most western businessmen are impatient. These businessmen come to China with a fixed time schedule. Hotels and air tickets are booked in advance. Meetings are arranged in advance down to the last minute. At least they think they are, that is, until they get off the airplane. That's when they realise they have really arrived in China.

This was what Richard H. Solomon, former Assistant Secretary of State to Henry Kissinger realised when he stepped off the plane at Beijing's Capital Airport in 1975. He arrived to negotiate a communique. Like most State Department officials, he arrived ready to "hit the ground running" and negotiate the kind of communique that would be full of all the "right stuff". Right? Not so!

The first thing on Solomon's agenda was not a negotiation. "They invited us out to a picnic in the Western Hills," Solomon recalled in later years. "Kissinger was going crazy."

The Chinese kept the entire American State Department delegation hanging at the edge trying to figure out what was next on the agenda. The Americans spent the entire time chomping at the bit waiting for some real negotiation to begin.

71

"The Chinese were dragging things out," described Solomon. Hoping that the Americans would give in rather than miss their self-imposed deadline, the Chinese waited until the last minute. "Then, they gave him (Kissinger) an unacceptable document at midnight on the last day of the visit."

All too often western businessmen come to China with big talk and too much anxiety to sign a contract, often without fully realising what they are plunging into.

When the Chinese party senses that its foreign counterpart is fixed to a deadline, half the battle is won. By simply bidding time, the Chinese party will often force the foreign side into a position where it is bargaining against itself.

One example of such a situation was when one American multinational innocently told the Chinese party that it wanted to be in full production by a certain date. The Chinese party simply dictated the terms from that point on. They gave the American party a standard form Chinese contract which had nothing to do with the deal at hand.

When the foreign party questioned the document, the Chinese folded their arms and casually explained that it was what the foreign party had to do if they in fact wanted to start production within their self-imposed time-frame. The Americans panicked and the Chinese had a field day at the negotiation table.

Strategy 20: Catching Fishes from Troubled Waters
(混水摸鱼)

Interpretation : Fishes feel lost and disillusioned in troubled waters; there-
fore, they become easy prey. Create a chaotic and panicky
situation, the adversary can neither think nor see clearly to
respond to the pressing situation.

During the Three Kingdoms Period, Liu Bei took advantage of the chaotic situation to take control over the city of Jinzhou. Liu Bei further took advantage of an internal struggle within the enemy camp to seize another strategic city.

America's giant corporation AT&T has had over a decade of floundering in troubled waters in China. The company's problems began in the early 1980s when China began shopping for advanced digital switching technology. While China looked to the US for technology, the AT&T shrugged off China (now the biggest market for telephones, switching equipments in the world — and expected to be so for the next thirty years) as strategically unimportant.

Surprise! While AT&T was unwilling to transfer top-line technology to China, France's Alcatel, Germany's Siemens, and Japan's NEC jumped into the market to become China's top three equipment suppliers. It was Alcatel, Siemens and NEC who caught fishes from the "troubled water" — China.

In the mid-1980s, when AT&T finally got around to realising that it could not rely on the US market alone, they plunged into the China market without the research and without knowing the telephone habits of the Chinese people. Access to telephones in China at that time were quite limited and the service generally poor. People often had to wait to use public telephones, and once they had a telephone in hand, had to wait to obtain a free line. Furthermore, to address the particular characteristics of the Chinese market, switches have to be engineered in a particular way.

AT&T however, thinking in a merrily American straightforward fashion, simply shipped its own off-the-shelf units to China. The first switch installed in Wuhan was quickly overwhelmed by overuse and could not meet the strain of the domestic market. Chinese consumers and telephone users complained to the Ministry of Posts and Telecommunications which in turn complained to AT&T through AT&T's office in Hong Kong. AT&T in trying to run a China operation had not even bothered to set up an office in China — another strategic mistake. The Hong Kong office could not fix the problems so AT&T had to order parts from the US, along with technicians and ship all these to China. Over the course of months, AT&T tried to resolve the problem which soon mushroomed in time into other problems with AT&T's switches elsewhere in China.

AT&T fell by the wayside as Alcatel and other competitors, which already had established offices with teams on the ground in China, were able to address their domestic problems with speed and efficiency. As one person close to the company explained, "AT&T thought that they could go in and sell switches like it was Iowa."

People familiar with AT&T's operations say that AT&T considered every sale a purely commercial transaction, while the Chinese on the other hand, looked to try and build, with each sale, foundations for a long-term business relationship. Disgusted with AT&T's attitude, the Chinese eventually stopped buying from them in the late 1980s.

At great expense AT&T's Vice Chairman Randy Tobbis spent two years in the 1990's shuttling back and forth between New York and Beijing trying to straighten out AT&T's mess. AT&T finally signed tentative agreements with Beijing which include plans for joint ventures to manufacture digital switches in China. It has now finally employed more than 400 people in China and it continues to add more today, in order to address its problems.

Strategy 21: The Cicada Sheds Its Shells (金蝉脱壳)

Interpretation : When escaping, do so secretly without making it public. Develop a false stronghold to deter the adversary from attacking, then withdraw secretly leaving an empty nest.

Lu Bu had served in Yuan Shao's army during the period of the Three Kingdoms; however, Yuan Shao had never completely trusted Lu Bu. Later, Lu Bu agreed to leave the service of Yuan Shao but Yuan Shao sent soldiers after Lu Bu with the aim of murdering him. Knowing Yuan Shao's distrust, Lu Bu created what looked like a sleeping person in his tent and slipped away and thus escaping death.

Sun Tze advocated, "When strong feint weakness." Often in China, one does not know who they are speaking with. Sharp American merchant bankers, or Hong Kong businessmen dressed to the teeth will often sneer at their Chinese counterparts who may appear at meetings in open collar shirts or even jeans.

The China of the 1990s is different from the China of the past two decades. While the Chinese may often still wear jeans and slippers to meetings, they carry handphones and drive in Mercedes, having in fact now adopted a new kind of sophistication which goes along with being the third largest economy in the world, and being among the top six nations in the world, possess the highest levels of foreign exchange reserves. Having issued bonds and listing on major stock markets in the world, Chinese-backed corporations are now entering the market in a way which was never expected a few years ago.

When cigarette smoke is suffocating and the ashes are piled up high in the saucers of tea and coffee cups scattered across the boardroom table, the Chinese and foreign party cannot see eye to eye on the key issues of the deal, and it becomes clear that the yin and yang symbiosis of what everyone thought would be a fruitful negotiation is about to head into a tail spin, it is time to seek an indirect route to solving the mess.

This may often mean changing venues, and putting everything onto a lighter note. It is often surprising for foreign investors to find negotiations cut-off at the pass as they are herded out of the negotiation room and into a restaurant or karaoke bar for further indirect discussions in a spirit more keen with "friendly discussions and mutual benefit."

Changing venue and putting things in another light is a critical game which could be played by both sides. When the foreign party finds that discussions are going nowhere, ending the discussions and moving to a dinner followed by karaoke in a hotel/nightclub would probably do more to reach some kind of mutual understanding on the issues than trying to thrash them out at the table. Furthermore, the Chinese negotiate collectively as a group. With a number of opinions which may differ slightly from each other, this makes it difficult to break through team pressure in trying to put forward an idea. Consequently, by moving the parties to another venue, it provides a much more relaxed atmosphere in which ideas can be put forward to individuals of the other team on a personal level to try to create some influence in their thinking and slowly adjust them to another position when everybody returns to the negotiation table again.

As one experienced negotiator explained, "When you go to the negotiation table in China, the Chinese will tell you that you must make certain concessions because they are a poor under-developed country. Just remember Japan once pleaded poverty."

Strategy 22: Fasten the Door to Catch a Thief
(关门捉贼)

Interpretation : To destroy a weak adversary completely, leave no loop-hole for escape; to use total encirclement. If you allow a weak adversary to escape, he may make a comeback in the future.

In 260 BC, Qin Kingdom was at war with the Zhao. Qin general Bai Qi ordered a small force to lure Zhao's commander, Zhao Kuo out. When Zhao Kuo pursued Qin's forces all the way to Changbi, he walked into a trap of encirclement that Bai Qi had planned. The Zhao soldiers were cut off from its supplies and reinforcement, and were completely destroyed.

Negotiating on the Chinese party's home turf can be frustrating. The Chinese party's management may be interrupted at any time by the various matters involving the operation of their enterprise, and at any time they may leave the negotiating room to take care of these things — sometimes leaving their foreign counterpart stuck at the table for days waiting for them to resume discussions.

For instance, one negotiation team found themselves stuck in the freezing conference room of a factory one winter trying to make headway with the Chinese party's negotiation team. Negotiations were interrupted by breakfast, lunch and dinner every day. Dinners always turned into massive *ganbei* sessions with fiery local brew. After dinner, the negotiation team would be herded into the factory's karaoke disco for frivolities until midnight. The Chinese negotiation team would split up, one half accompanying the foreign team to dinner, drinking and disco-karaoke, while the other half slept early in pre-paration for the next day's negotiation. This way the Chinese side was always fresh and the foreign side always worn out.

To get control of the situation, the foreign team invited the Chinese team to a neutral city — Beijing — for negotiations. The foreign side booked the Chinese party's hotel rooms, arranged their meals, and fixed times for negotiation sessions so that the negotiations could keep on track. The Chinese were stuck. As long as the foreign side continued to pay their hotel and meal bills, they had to stay at the negotiation table and finish the deal.

Strategy 23: Befriend a Distant State While Attacking a Neighbouring State (远交近攻)

Interpretation : Adversaries at a distance can be a temporal ally. Do not attempt to take on too many enemies at any one time. Another similar idiom states that a far away water supply is no good in saving a nearby fire. The immediate danger needs to be taken care of first. If there is no short term, there is no longer term to consider.

During the Warring States Period, an able counsel, Fan Sui advised the Qin Emperor to conquer neighbouring states first while establishing a friendship with distant states. The Qin Emperor, Zhao Qin, heeded Fan Sui's advice and made him prime minister. The Qin kingdom then defeated Han, Zhao, Wei, Chu, Yan and then finally Qi and for the first time in history unified China.

Despite 2,000 yards of central border friction between China and Vietnam, during the war of resistance in Vietnam against the American forces (1960s–1970s), China was a great support to the Vietnamese government and military. High level Vietnamese officials were entertained in Beijing throughout the 1960s, and Chinese technical experts supported the Vietcong both behind the frontlines and sometimes in the field as well.

During the long war in Indochina against the Americans, from their stronghold positions in both Laos, Cambodia as well as in south Vietnam, the Communist Parties of the three Indochina countries were so close that Ho Chi Minh spoke of their relations as being as close as "lips and teeth."

In 1979, the juxtaposition of relationships changed completely. With Saigon safely liberated by the Vietcong and renamed Ho Chi Minh City, and Phnom Penh under Khmer Rouge control, the united front of Indochina began to crack. The Vietnamese Communist Party and the Khmer Rouge could not see eye to eye on a number of policies relating to economic reform as well as territorial control.

When Pol Pot introduced his policy of Year Zero, complemented by a policy of genocide of Vietnamese living in Cambodia (later to extend to approximately one million of his own people), Vietnam and Cambodia relations broke. At the same time, however, China feeling growing tension between itself and Vietnam extended a hand to the Khmer Rouge. Pol Pot's first public appearance ever outside of the jungles of Cambodia was in fact at Beijing Capital Airport when he was met by Hua Guo Feng in 1970.

When the Khmer Rouge attacked the Vietnamese border in the south in 1979, the Vietnamese counter-attacked. Entering Cambodia, the Vietnamese troops discovered one mass grave after another and realising the mess in which Cambodia had become, marched on into Phnom Penh kicking Pol Pot out and across to the Thai border.

China responded by attacking Vietnam to "teach the Vietnamese a lesson" but not without first befriending the distant Khmer Rouge state.

The tragic war of 1979 between China and Vietnam left many dead on both sides, and the new alignment with Chinese–Vietnamese relations broken, and China extending enormous support to the Khmer Rouge, who continued to fight from their jungle hideouts along the Thai border.

This spread out Vietnam's own military resources leaving Vietnam stretched on two fronts and much of its economic resources being channelled into defence. Unable to continue with its financial resources over-extended, Vietnam had to eventually retreat from Cambodia. In 1992, Party-to-Party relations were more or less patched between China and Vietnam, and today they enjoy a tremendous border trade.

Strategy 24: Borrow a Safe Passage to Conquer the Kingdom of Guo (假途灭虢)

Interpretation : Help the weak when the weak is not threatening so as to win over their support. Mere talk will not save the weak; action speaks louder than words.

During the Spring and Autumn Period, Jin had always wanted to conquer the kingdoms of Guo and Yu. Xun Xi, an advisor of Jin suggested that the emperor of Yu should be bribed into allowing Jin forces to pass through the state of Yu to attack Guo. Yu greedily and foolishly agreed. Guo was subsequently invaded but the Jin turned around and destroyed Yu as well.

China has traditionally adopted a diplomatic policy of separating state-to-state from Party-to-Party relations.

In this regard, for many years China maintained diplomatic relations with the governments of various countries while at the same time supporting the communist parties in those countries pushing their own policy platforms which were often different from those of the government themselves.

This was the case in Indonesia and Malaysia where China maintained diplomatic relations with the governments concerned and at the same time, supported the communist party in each place which had their own separate agenda against the government.

In other matters, China has championed the third world and developing nations in providing support for both revolutionary as well as development causes in many of these countries.

Shortly after World War II, when North Korea broke into fighting, it was a decision of China to support North Korea even though this caused enormous losses for China. It was the dedication to helping brother socialist countries in their time of need which became a major policy platform of China. At the same time, of course, China obtained strategic access through such assistance.

Likewise, during the Vietnam War, China sent a number of advisors to North Vietnam and provided great assistance and support in both the liberation of North Vietnam from the French and the liberation of South Vietnam from the Americans. China also provided assistance to the Pathet Lao in their own war of liberation and later even to the Khmer Rouge in Cambodia. While helping the weak in these situations, China also gained strategic access and a greater sphere of allegiances and influence in the regions bordering China.

Strategy 25: Steal the Beams and Pillars and Replace Them with Rotten Timber (偷梁換柱)

Interpretation : To sabotage, incapacitate, or destroy your adversary by removing his key support.

During the reign of Emperor Zheng Zong of the Song Dynasty, the Empress was upset because one of the Emperor's courtesans was pregnant while she was not. Feeling that her rightful position as Empress might be threatened if the courtesan has a boy, she devised a scheme, and pretended that she was pregnant by sticking a pillow under her dress. When the courtesan finally did deliver a boy, the Empress had one of her trusted servants sneakily steal the boy and replace it with a pussy cat.

The British are masters at applying this strategy to the colonies which they are about to dispose. In India, Fiji, Malaysia, and Singapore, they drained the financial resources of the place, and mixed up the local ethnic population. This was the colonial inheritance.

Today in Hong Kong, with 1997 only two years away, the situation is not much different. One can clearly see an established pattern of colonial departure taking shape.

Having a clear perspective on the colonial history of their neighbours, this is exactly what the Chinese are afraid of — that the British colonialists will "replace the pillars" of the Hong Kong Government "with rotten timber" before returning it to China.

For instance, the thing that seems to be of greatest interest to the British Government in its negotiations with China is the building of an enormous airport. Designated to be located on an island in the middle of the sea far away from everything else in Hong Kong, requiring massive infrastructure investment to build all road and rail links to it, it is seen by many to be a white elephant. The Chinese think that the need for the airport is questionable given the fact that international airports now exist in Macao, Shenzhen, Zhuhai, Guangzhou, not to mention the existing facility in Hong Kong.

Nevertheless, the British have insisted at great lengths on pushing the project through. Some suggested that the intention is to use the bulk of Hong Kong's remaining foreign exchange reserves to dish out contracts to British construction companies tendering for the project. With Hong Kong empty of foreign exchange reserves, it is not all that certain how useful the new airport will be.

Similarly, the British have fought for a "through train" government. This means that the terms of the current members of the Legislative Counsel will span 1997. China's concern is that it will inherit more "rotten timbers" in the woodwork of the Hong Kong Government.

Strategy 26: Point at the Mulberry but Curse the Locust
(指桑骂槐)

Interpretation : To make use of a subject as a pretext to express one's objections.

During the regime of Emperor Xianzong of the Ming Dynasty, there was an evil eunuch named Wang Zhi. Wang Zhi was very close to the Emperor and had assumed a lot of power which had made him a very dangerous man and not good for the Ming Dynasty.

One day, an actor in the imperial court named A Chou gave a performance before the imperial court in which he portrayed a drunkard. When acting as a drunkard, he made many comments freely. As part of the performance, suddenly he was warned to stop his singing and acting as a high-ranking Mandarin was approaching the area of the performance. A Chou replied, "I am not afraid of a high-ranking mandarin" and kept dancing and continued making jokes. Next he heard a warning that the Emperor himself would be passing by. He continued making jokes and indicating that he was not even afraid of the Emperor. Then a warning came that the eunuch Wang Zhi would be approaching. A Chou suddenly fell to his knees and said, "Death penalty is my desert(s)! Death penalty is my desert! I am not afraid of the Emperor, but I am afraid of Eunuch Wang Zhi." Under this circumstance, by expressing his fear in the eunuch more than in the Emperor, A Chou was indirectly letting everybody know that Wang Zhi was a dangerous man and even the Emperor should be careful and in a subtle way, "cursed" criticised the Emperor of his foolishness to distinguish those faithful subordinates from the evil ones.

The use of the strategy (to Point at the Mulberry but Curse the Locust) means to borrow or use one thing to achieve another end.

A good example of this strategy is the current ongoing US-China trade dispute.

"Point at the mulberry and curse the locust" is an ancient Chinese proverb, but it is one that the United States Government's trade negotiators have learned well. Translated into not-so-oblique language, it might go: "Point at the US trade deficit and curse China's foreign exchange system and China's failure to protect intellectual property rights."

Lacking better tools with which to negotiate reducing America's ballooning trade deficit with China — it reached US$17.6 billion for the first eight months of the year 1994 — the US has pressed ahead with its negative campaign. Last summer, Treasury Under Secretary Lawrence Summers accused China of manipulating its foreign exchange system to prevent an effective balance of payments adjustment. He threatened to prevent China's entry into the General Agreement on Tariffs and Trade (GATT) if the situation was not corrected.

Strategy 27: Play Dumb (装聋作哑)

Interpretation : To let your adversary underestimate your capabilities.

During the Three Kingdoms Period, Sima Yi played dumb so as to let Cao Shuang think that he was weak, ill and useless. Sima Yi however, used the opportunity to catch Cao Shuang off-guard and kill him, thereby taking command himself.

The worst mistake anyone can make in a negotiation in China is to underestimate the opposition. Western negotiators arriving in China in their sharp business suits and branded suspenders, often sneer when they enter the negotiating room to find their counterparts wearing jeans and slippers, and smoking endless rounds of cigarettes.

While the Chinese party may not look as slick as their foreign western counterparts, they may know a lot more about the west than the westerners whom they are dealing with know or even can imagine about China.

During the late 70s, China was coming out of the cultural revolution, and during the 80s, it entered a new era of economic growth. In those days, western imports were new, and westerners found it easy business to impress their counterparts by simply being western.

In 1988, a Hong Kong delegation of businessmen visited Shanghai and to their surprise found the Vice Mayor showing up for the meeting in a pair of hiking boots (probably having just come from inspecting some site). The Hong Kong businessmen with their impressive Rolex watches sniggered among themselves, whispering in imitated British accents "Oh, how terrible! Look at the way the Vice Mayor dresses. Simply terrible!" They did not realise that Zhu Rongji, then Vice Mayor, would become first Vice Premier only five years later, and the "financial czar" of China instituting some of the most progressive financial reforms that the country has ever seen.

While foreign managers bring their operational techniques and analytical abilities, they often hit a brick wall as they enter the China market for not being able to understand the distribution and sales tricks which their

Chinese counterparts have so successfully developed in order to overcome inter-provincial protectionism and a market where relations *guanxi* are all important in cracking the domestic market.

Even though western businessmen may be flashing out statistics on fanciful calculators, they may be making unrealistic predictions for sales volume and profit, which are not possible to achieve in the China market without adopting the kind of "backdoor" techniques which the Chinese have developed to use as a matter of survival (like using State-subsidised raw materials and goods to undercut market prices).

Strategy 28: Remove the Ladder after Your Ascent
(上屋抽梯)

Interpretation : To lure an adversary into a trap, and then cut him off.

This strategy comes from the Three Kingdoms Period, when a young warlord was caught in a family feud and sought the advice of the master strategist Zhuge Liang, who really did not want to get involved in a family dispute. Nevertheless, Zhuge Liang reluctantly went to visit the young warlord, but still refused to get involved in the feud.

The warlord cleverly invited Zhuge Liang to visit his library upstairs to see his collection of rare and classic books. Zhuge Liang complied only to find that the ladder had been removed after ascending to the library. He himself had been outwitted. With no way out, he agreed to advise the young warlord.

Mao Zedong adopted the strategy of "luring the enemy in deep, avoiding his main force and striking at his weak spots."

Again and again, Mao Zedong employed this strategy in luring Chiang Kaishek's troops deep into "Red base" areas, and trapping them when they pushed "straight ahead" and in too deep. Mao Zedong described this strategy, citing a scene in the classical novel *Outlaws of the Marsh*. Mao wrote:

> "We all know that when two boxers fight, the clever boxer usually gives a little ground at first, while the foolish one rushes in furiously and uses up his resources at the very start, and in the end he is often beaten by the man who has given ground. In the novel, *Outlaws of the Marsh*, the drill master Hang, challenging Lin Chong to fight on Chai Jin's estate, shouts 'Come on! Come on!' In the end, it is the retreating Lin Chong who spots Hang's weak point and floors him with one blow."

That was what happened to one Jardine Matheson Holdings Ltd. employee who went to Xianfan in the middle of winter to finalise contract discussions for the purchase of ball bearings. To his surprise, the factory manager jacked up the price.

The haggling was to no avail. As the Jardine Matheson employee recalled later, "It was freezing cold, and the guest house at the factory had no hot water and no shower. I wore gloves in the dining room."

When it became clear to the Jardine Matheson employee that the haggling would go nowhere, he decided to leave town. At least he thought he could decide to leave town. Surprise. The factory officials told the Jardine Matheson employee, "Sorry, we can't help you get a train ticket." Then the employee decided to get transport to the train station to see if he might have better luck buying a ticket directly on his own. "Sorry," explained the factory officials, "Our shuttle bus is busy with other matters." The employee had no choice but to stay put. The shuttle bus remained "busy" for a few more days in the hopes that the employee would agree to the new price terms. He didn't. So one day, the Chinese factory sent the shuttle bus to take the frozen Jardine man to the train station to leave. Probably for good.

Strategy 29: Decorate the Tree with Fake Blossoms
（树上开花）

Interpretation : To exaggerate in order to mislead your adversary, letting him believe that you are very strong.

Emperor Yangdi of the Sui Dynasty built the Grand Canal in order to strengthen China's economy. At the same time, he went overboard to impress foreign visitors by ordering restaurants not to charge them for meals and to tell the travellers that "China is so rich that people don't need to pay for their meals." In the winter, he had the bear trees around the capital at Loyang decorated with silk flowers. However, upon leaving Loyang, the travellers could see the harsh reality of the countryside, and would realise after all that the silk flowers were just for show.

When tourists arrive in China, they are often welcomed by swarms of kindergarten children waving little flags and singing songs of welcome. When foreign investors arrive, they are taken on factory visits, shown well-organised production teams, and well-orchestrated demonstrations of government support for the factory concerned (which often includes local government leaders singing praises of the enterprise and acknowledging the preferential treatments available if the foreigners invest there).

The Chinese are masters at putting on a great show for their guests. When heads of State visit, crowds are mobilised to cheer, streets are cleaned and the impression is guaranteed to be deep.

When the Chairman of the Board of a foreign multinational comes to China, he is often greeted with VIP treatment at Beijing's Capital Airport with Mercedes Benz and police escort to the cavernous Great Hall of the People outfitted with its red carpets, and some of the most outlandish and expensive pieces of Chinese art. This however, is a far cry from the reality of managing State workers at a factory floor, which the CEO's company may be about to invest in. As one foreign company representative commented, "The last thing you want is for your CEO to come to China on a whirlwind trip, get enchanted, make promises, and leave you to negotiate the details."

Strategy 30: Turn Yourself into a Host from Being a Guest (反客为主)

Interpretation : To exchange place/position; reverse the situation.

When Liu Bang and Xiang Yu led a successful rebellion against the Qin Emperor, Liu Bang entered the Imperial Palace first, while Xiang Yu (who possessed the bigger force) was busy with mopping up operations in the provinces. As Liu Bang was about to settle down to his first evening in the Palace with the toppled Emperor's retinue of concubines, an advisor warned that Xiang Yu had almost four times as many troops and that Liu Bang should be careful as he was only a "guest" and that Xiang Yu would be the real "host" when he returned.

Liu Bang, taking his tip, left the Palace. Xiang Yu came back and got besotted with concubines and Palace pleasures. Meanwhile, Liu Bang built up his forces, and when strong enough returned to kick Xiang Yu out of the Palace (Xiang Yu and his favourite courtesan both slit their own throats as they were fleeing).

Turning yourself into a host from being a guest is a classic strategy for reversing positions and turning the situation upside down.

Tired of having to *ganbei* through banquet after banquet with officials in China, Karl Heinz Ege, a German representative who has been living in China for four years finally decided to bring a bottle of German Schnapps to banquets. When the Maotai *ganbei*ing situation got out of control, Karl Ege would pull the bottle of Schnapps out from a paper bag he kept under the table and begin filling up the glasses of his host with Schnapps, insisting that they must try "German Maotai". The officials winced and grimaced one by one as they forced the Schnapps down their throats. Faces turned red and then white. The toasting ritual subdued into a mild exchange of courtesies.

The most classic example of being turned from a guest into a host occurred when one European company seeking to obtain the support of the provincial government decided to go on a lobbying mission to meet the

Governor of the province. The Managing Director of the European company however, insisted to his staff that "This was to be a serious meeting" and "that there is to be no banqueting or drinking with the Chinese officials", and "we must be serious and make them know that we are serious about the issues at hand."

When the managers on the ground were arranging for their boss to arrive for the meetings, the provincial government's foreign affairs office (expecting the foreign party to host the dinner, of course) asked, "For the dinner you are hosting for the Governor, do you want to book the restaurant or should we book it for you?" The staff too embarrassed to explain their boss's view on the subject, simply let the provincial government make the arrangements. When the Managing Director of the European company arrived to meet with the Governor of the province for "serious formal discussions", the meeting lasted fifteen minutes. The Governor simply explained, "I support your project, now let's go have dinner and drink."

The European company's Managing Director then found out that he was hosting dinner for a number of provincial government officials who consumed several bottles of XO and exotic (and expensive) bear's paw at the expense of their foreign company. The foreign party then found to their surprise that the provincial government also hit them with a bill for renting the meeting room for their meeting with the Governor!

Strategy 31: Use a Beauty to Ensnare a Man (美人计)

Interpretation : To intoxicate or indulge your adversary with a time/energy absorbing activity thereby diminishing his spirit to fight.

During the Eastern Han Dynasty, the Prime Minister Dong Zhuo was a debauched tyrant, ruling for the boy Emperor. One court official Wang Yun, thought of a master plan to defeat Dong Zhuo.

Wang Yun collaborated with his beautiful daughter in the plot. Wang promised his daughter to both Dong Zhuo as well as Lu Bu, Dong Zhuo's loyal Commander-General of the military, at the same time. The daughter used her charms to charm both equally. Dong Zhuo as Prime Minister ordered Lu Bu to keep his hands off the daughter. Lu Bu as commander of the military killed Dong Zhuo. Wang's daughter smiled.

This is the oldest trick in the book. The Chinese love sending sprite 20-year-olds to accompany middle aged and up executives as translators to their meetings. It makes the executives talk. The translators just need to listen.

This is also an easy strategy for the Chinese party to adopt in getting rid of the foreign manager of a joint venture if they want a quick replacement, but are too polite to voice their views openly at a board meeting. Foreign managers hanging out in China alone for too long are prone to weakness, an easy pickup, and an easier nab by the police.

When found with a prostitute, the police will stamp the word "prostitute" on every page of a foreigner's passport and ignominiously send him off at the nearest airport. One Australian executive was so proud at having been arrested in China for a "sexual offence" that he had his red-chopped passport framed.

Strategy 32: Open the Gate of an Undefended City
(空城计)

Interpretation : To generate doubts in adversary's camp by presenting some-thing that is really simple; let the adversary overestimate your capabilities.

During the Three Kingdoms Period, master statesman and strategist, Zhuge Liang, upon seeing his city-fortress surrounded by hostile and overwhelming enemy troops, created this strategy by opening wide the gates of the besieged city, showing the enemy forces the empty streets within, seemingly disarmed with only dustsweepers brushing the dust away from the open gate. Fearing a trick, the enemy immediately retreated, and gave up the plan to besiege the city.

Tours to model factories and words of "everything is OK" or "no problem" often do more to scare away investors than attract them.

Western businessmen often plough through their negotiations with the Chinese party sitting on the other side at the table nodding their heads, without realising that the Chinese party may not have agreed to any of the conditions or terms which the foreign businessmen are ticking off as they go through their contract assuming that agreement has been obtained from the other side.

As mentioned earlier in this book, "yes" in China can be a broad interpretation for a number of responses from the Chinese party but which in fact may really mean "Yes, I will think about it" or even better, "It sounds OK." (Refer to Part II: The Art of Saying "Yes" for a list of possible positive responses given by the Chinese during a negotiation.)

Take for instance, the foreign party entering into a technology transfer agreement which sat all night with the governor of the city and the Chinese party at a banquet. They were so convinced that the deal was had, and returned to Beijing to tell their lawyers to write up the contracts because "the governor kept nodding his head throughout the dinner." Therefore, he must be supporting their projects. The Chinese factory Chairman mentioned to them afterwards that "everything was OK and that there was no problem." But in fact, this just means that "Based on the present situation, everything *should* be OK and that there *should* be no problem. But, as time goes on, there may be alot of (new) problems arising, so the terms and conditions agreed upon earlier should be discussed again (and again) when the time comes for the occasion. (Please note the "But's" after their "Yes's.")

Strategy 33: Use Adversary's Spies to Sow Discord in Your Adversary's Camp (反间计)

Interpretation : To spread wrong information; sow distrust or dissension among your adversaries; sow distrust or discord among one's enemies through one's counterespionage.

During the Three Kingdoms Period, Zhou Yu used Cao Cao's spy to give misinformation to Cao Cao, leading Cao Cao to kill his own able navy commanders. This left Cao Cao without anyone qualified to command his fleet of ships, which soon met disaster.

Sun Tze advocated manipulating the enemy's agents to serve your own objectives.

This is a favourite game of both foreign investors who often deliberately discuss garbage over tapped telephones and those Chinese counterparts who reveal false intentions through attractive translators wearing the latest imported catwalk costume.

One foreign businessman who came to China with preconceived ideas about Chinese commercial espionage, was convinced that the old hotel dating from the 1950s in which he was staying had a bug somewhere in the old Soviet architecture. He literally tore up his hotel room searching for the bug, which he was convinced must be there.

Finally under the large Chinese carpet which dominated the room, he found a round metal plate with three screws fastening it to the floor. This must be the bug! He quickly took a coin out of his pocket and unscrewed the first screw. He then unscrewed the second screw. He was excited at the adventurous thought of finally discovering and exposing the bug planted in his room as he began to unscrew the third — only to have his anticipation dissipated when he heard the old Soviet-style chandelier in the room below crash to the floor.

Strategy 34: Inflict Pain on Oneself in order to Infiltrate Adversary's Camp and Win the Confidence of the Enemy (苦肉计)

Interpretation : To absorb loss in order to win trust; inflicting an injury on oneself to win confidence.

During the Spring and Autumn Period, the king of Zheng in a stratagem to lower the resolve of his enemy the king of Hu, gave his favourite daughter to the king of Hu in marriage. In order to show his goodwill toward Hu, he then executed one of his own advisors who had advocated attacking Hu. Seeing all this, the king of Hu trusted that his border with the kingdom of Zheng would be safe from invasion. At that point, Zheng launched a surprise attack against Hu and conquered the kingdom outright.

An assassin who attempted to kill the first Emperor, Qin Shi Huangdi, cut off his best friend's head (who was on the Emperor's "wanted list") so as to gain an audience with the Emperor himself.

Foreign investors will often be impressed by the expenses to which their Chinese hosts will go to impress them with banquets, trips to local sightseeing places, and gifts. "Of course we trust our hosts ... they paid for everything," says the naive investor. Beware!

Many overseas Chinese returning to China, come first as bearers of gifts before they ask for something in return. They will often donate some of their money earned overseas to building schools, roads and hospitals in the communities from which their parents or grandparents came.

While on the surface this may be seen as an act of goodwill and great benevolence, it is in fact a strategic move. These overseas Chinese by donating to the community from which their ancestors came, are not only developing good relations with the officials who are in charge today, but creating a subtle kind of obligation which these officials have to repay in supporting their investment project which will come to the table later on. In this manner, money spent as a loss on donations and gifts, returns later when one needs something done.

Strategy 35: Lead Your Adversary to Chain Together Their Warships (连环计)

Interpretation : *To turn your adversary's strength into weakness; lead your adversary on until they fall by their pride; now also means, a set of interlocking stratagems (series of stratagems) leading your adversary to defeat.*

This strategy comes from the Three Kingdoms Period when General Cao Cao was ill-advised into chaining his ships together before ferrying troops across a river on the claim that this would give the boats more stability when crossing the turbulent river. Cao Cao found to his dismay that the enemy had intended for him to do this, so that when they lit his ships on fire, they would be linked together with iron chains and burnt as one.

When doing business in China, don't "chain your ships together." Also don't tie your own hands, or let your company headquarters get you all tied up either.

This same mistake was made when one multinational sent a Taiwanese manager to China with full responsibility to negotiate the deal on the simplistic assumption that because he spoke Mandarin he would have some knowledge of how to deal with the Chinese in China. Corporate headquarters was confident of its choice. Surprise!

The Taiwanese manager, concerned with covering his backside, was in hypertensive gear from day one and basically acted in the kind of pushy manner which may suit one trying to drive through Taipei rush hour traffic, but which will not save one's rear end at a negotiation table in China.

The negotiation began with the Taiwanese making his first mistake by demanding all kinds of controls over the Chinese management. This was not a good idea since it was the Chinese management who were negotiating with him. Corporate headquarters liked this kind of tough approach, and insisted that he maintain this line of attack at the negotiation table.

The second mistake was to present the Chinese management with a contract so tightly worded that even if the Chinese management was stupid, there would be no doubt that this joint venture was going to oust them from their seat of power, if not to castrate them in the sitting position. Corporate headquarters liked this kind of contract as it was drafted by American lawyers. They insisted that no changes be made at the negotiation table without clearance from lawyers back home.

The Company's third mistake was when he actually showed up in China thinking that he would actually get the Chinese party to sign the contract and agree to the castration terms. All corporate eyes in headquarters were on the Taiwanese manager waiting tensely for him to close the deal as quickly as possible. In fact, the deal was supposed to be closed before the end of the year to fit in neatly into that year's annual budget. The Christmas holidays were coming up. Everyone was waiting for a result. All hopes for the deal and decisions from the corporate side were inextricably linked.

"Clank" is the sound of a wad of tobacco being spit into an aluminium spittoon. When the Taiwanese heard this sound, he should have realised it would be a long negotiation.

Strategy 36: Retreat is the Best Option (走为上计)

Interpretation : Opting out; not participating/not playing the game that your adversary wants you to play.

During the Spring and Autumn Period, the king of Yue conquered the kingdom of Wu. The two men who had stood by the king of Yue's side and contributed to his cause were Fan Li and Wen Zhong. Fan Li however, decided to abstain from politics, and went into business. Wen Zhong however, followed the king of Yue to power, only to find that the king later had him killed because he was afraid that Wen Zhong might turn on him one day. The moral of the story is "he who runs away today, lives to do business another day."

As Mao Zedong said, "If the battle can be won, fight it; if not, depart."

As one China trader reminisced, "When the Chinese want you to sign a contract in a hurry, they always tell you there is another party who wants to do the deal with them, but 'because of their good relationship, they will give you first opportunity.' When they told me this in Shanghai, and showed me the terms, all I could say was if you have someone else who is actually willing to agree to these prices, as a 'friend', all I can say is you better get them to sign up as quickly as possible. I certainly can't accept these terms and I don't know anyone else who would. They just went into silent shock."

One lawyer was locked in three weeks of negotiations in Beijing. His driver (who likes to drive him to meetings because sometimes he gave him cigarettes) was very frustrated because the lawyer spent three weeks locked in meetings and never come out. Finally, the driver left a message with the lawyer's secretary in his Beijing office, "Tell your clients that if they can't make money in China; then just go home!"

Annex

CHINESE DYNASTIES CHRONOLOGY

Xia (21st–16th Centuries BC)

The legendary first dynasty of China. It is unclear what happened then, but people believe that the I-Ching was developed during this period.

Shang (16th–11th Centuries BC)

A prosperous period, famous for bronzes and pottery.

Western Zhou (11th Century–770 BC)

Chinese culture began to ascend during this period. Written records remain intact. Law, education and ethics develop to new heights.

Eastern Zhou (770–256 BC)

Replaces Western Zhou and written records, education and ethics move from western China to eastern China. Eventually the whole thing collapses and the Spring and Autumn Period begins.

Spring and Autumn Period (722–481 BC)

Not to be confused with the Spring and Autumn Festivals in China.

Warring States Period (403–221 BC)

China was divided into many small kingdoms which fought against each other. Most of the stories contained in this book come from this period.

Qin (221–206 BC)

The first Emperor of China unified the country by defeating all of the states fighting among each other during the Warring States Period. He did so by adopting many of the strategies mentioned in this book. He built the Great Wall to prevent people outside of China from adopting these strategies and using them against him. He was buried among a complete pottery replication of his army known as the "Terra Cotta Warriors" which is a statement to his prowess and successful utilisation of the strategies contained in this book, and is a famous tourist site in China today (responsible for bringing a great amount of foreign exchange into the country).

Western Han (206 BC–AD 9)

After the first Emperor died, nobody could step into his shoes, and other people adopted the strategies contained in this book and kicked out the status quo. A new dynasty emerged called the Western Han. The story of Liu Bang, the first Emperor of this dynasty is contained in this book.

Xin (AD 9–23)

A period of economic growth and stability in China. In the absence of fighting, most of the strategies contained in this book were not used and saved for the Eastern Han Dynasty (see below).

Eastern Han (25–220)

The calm of the Xin erupted in the chaos of the Eastern Han. Strategy 31 came from this period. The chaos eventually got out of hand and China was divided into three kingdoms (see below).

Three Kingdom (220–265)
(Wei, Shu, Wu)

This was a period when China was split into three kingdoms which warred against each other and became the basis of China's epic, the "Romance of the Three Kingdoms." Most of the strategies contained in this book which do not come from the Warring States Period come from this period. The "Romance of the Three Kingdoms" became a classic text of strategy. Aside from Sun Tze's *Art of War*, Mao Zedong adopted many of his own strategies from this epic.

Western Jin (265–316)

This was a period of economic retraction and consolidation of assets by the power elite. People did not like it however, and the Western Jin were replaced by the Eastern Jin (see below).

Eastern Jin (317–420)

This was a period of great military might because a new power elite kicked out the former power elite of the Western Jin (see above) using some of the strategies contained in this book.

Northern and Southern Dynasties (386–581)
(Song, Qi, Liang, Chen, Northern Wei,
Eastern Wei, Western Wei, Northern Zhou)

China was divided into many different kingdoms which fought against each other. Some of the strategies in this book were used during this period. Others were invented during this period. It was during this period that the compass was invented in China.

Shui (581–618)

The Great Canal was dug during this dynasty. It is still being used today. In fact some think it is more efficient than flying local planes in China and safer as well.

Tang (611–907)

One of China's most glorious dynasties. Great cultural heights were obtained. Famous pottery horses were made, replicas of which can now be purchased in most Friendship Stores in China. Great poetry was written second only to that of the Song (see following page).

Five Dynasties (907–960)
(Later Liang, Later Tang, Later Jin, Later Han, Later Zhou)

As soon as one Emperor consolidated power, another kicked him out (using the strategies in this book).

Northern Song (960–1127)

Before the Song were pushed south they were known as the Northern Song.

Southern Song (1127–1279)

Famous for their poetry, the Songs were too busy with prose to do anything about the growing Mongol threat on their northern border. The result was that they were conquered (see below).

Yuan (1279–1368)

After Ghengis Khan conquered Europe, his grandson Kublai felt bored trashing knights wearing aluminium cans over their heads and wanted something more challenging. The result was that the Mongols attacked the Southern Song in China, and took over the middle kingdom. During this period, Marco Polo visited China, bought gunpowder, and civilised Europe.

Ming (1368–1644)

Famous for pottery (white and blue), the Ming reached one of the highest stages of cultural sophistication in China. While simple in decor, their furniture make a great buy for any antique collector who has a chance to obtain a real one.

Qing (1644–1911)

The last Dynasty and last Emperor. Antiques from this period can be legally exported from China.